AGGRESSION IN YOUTH

Violence is endemic in modern society; it is now a major sociomedical issue. Nor is the problem confined to adults: aggression in schools causes genuine anxiety and fear among teachers. Changing social and family patterns are everywhere raising hostility ratings among the young. It is little use retreating into bewilderment at the outward signs of their aggression. We need to know more of the underlying motives which lead youngsters to smash shop windows or wreck children's playgrounds. Roy Ridgway, a medical journalist and himself a family man, made it his job to find out. He became professionally involved with young people, and talked to them on their own ground. This book is the product of his researches. In it he analyses some of the deeper emotions behind the actions of many young people. It suggests new yardsticks by which parents, teachers and social workers can help young people, first to understand themselves better, and then to grow up as happier, more integrated personalities.

PRIORY EDITORIAL CONSULTANTS

THE CARE AND WELFARE LIBRARY

Consultant Medical Editor: Alexander R. K. Mitchell, MB,
ch.B, MRCPE, MRCPsych.

AGGRESSION
IN YOUTH

ROY RIDGWAY

with an additional section by

RONALD GIBSON, CBE, MA, LL.D, FRCS.
General Practitioner and a Medical Officer to
Winchester College and St. Swithun's School, Winchester

Foreword by
THE REV. THE LORD SOPER

PRIORY PRESS LIMITED

The Care and Welfare Library

The Alcoholic and the Help He Needs   Max M. Glatt, MD, FRCPsych., MRCP, DPM

Drugs—The Parents' Dilemma   Alexander R. K. Mitchell, MB, ch.B, MRCPE, MRCPsych.

Schizophrenia   Alexander R. K. Mitchell, MB, ch.B, MRCPE, MRCPsych.

Sex and the Love Relationship   Faith Spicer, MB, BS, JP

Sexually Transmitted Diseases   Roy Statham, MB, ch.B

The Child Under Stress   Edna Oakshott, OBE, BSC., ph.D

Stress in Industry   Joseph L. Kearns, MB, BCh., MSC.

Student Health   Philip Cauthery, MB, ch.B, DPh.

The Slow to Learn   James Ellis, M.Ed.

I.Q.-150   Sydney Bridges, MA, M.Ed., ph.D

When Father is Away   The Rev. A. H. Denney, AKC, BA

Healing Through Faith   Christopher Woodward, MRCS, LRCP

The Care of the Dying   Richard Lammerton, MRCS, LRCP

Health in Middle Age   Michael Green, MA, MB, BCh.

Easier Childbirth   R. E. Robinson, FRCS, and B. R. Wilkie, BM, BCh.

Migraine   Edda Hanington, MB, BS

Children in Hospital   Ann Hales-Tooke, MA

Depression—The Blue Plague   C. A. H. Watts, OBE, MD

SBN 85078 053 5 (Paperback)
    85078 052 7 (Hardback)
Copyright © 1973 by Roy Ridgway
First published in 1973 by
Priory Press Limited
101 Grays Inn Road London WC1
Made and printed in Great Britain by
The Garden City Press Limited
Letchworth, Hertfordshire SG6 1JS

Contents

To the young people I know best—Michael, Penny, Tony, Stephen, Alex, Daryl, Erika and Dacia.

Acknowledgements

THIS book could not have been written without the help and inspiration of a great many people, living and dead, who are too numerous to mention here: parents, friends, psychologists, philosophers and preachers, but of the latter, I would like to mention Dr. F. W. Dwelly, the first Dean of Liverpool Cathedral, whose Congregational services I attended regularly as an adolescent myself and who was a very great influence in my life—and his friend, Dr. Charles Raven, whose teaching I have never forgotten and can be summed up in one sentence: "Love, and not force, is the ultimate power in the universe."

In the actual writing of the manuscript, I must mention a number of people to whom I am greatly indebted. My wife, Dorothea, has been a great help with the interviewing. Everything I have written in this book she has heard; and this I believe is the best way to help any writer, because words that cannot be spoken cannot, in my opinion, be true. I am also grateful to the Richmond Fellowship and to the young people in their hostels in Richmond and Southampton, and particularly to Mike Pegg, the warden of Lancaster House, for all the help they have given me. For the quotations from teenage essays I am indebted to Robin Robinson of the Bloxham Project Research Unit in Oxford; for the lyric expression of adolescent conflict in the Beatle songs, I acknowledge the work of Dr. L. Satiago whose paper on the subject appeared in the American magazine *Adolescence* (Summer, 1969).

I wish to thank Dr. Ronald Gibson, CBE, a very wise and good-humoured general practitioner, for his valuable contribution at the end of my book; the boys of Leighton Park School,

Aggression in Youth

Reading, for their essays on aggression; and last, but by no means least, Dr. Geoffrey Eley of Priory Press for his encouragement, infinite patience and expert guidance, and for very firmly preventing me from taking off (as I am apt to do) into the realms of abstract philosophy and pinning me down to saying things that I hope will be of practical help to all those concerned with the problem of aggression and violence in youth.

Foreword

by The Rev. The Lord Soper

A conjunction of the issues of youth and aggression (with its most characteristic expression in violence) in a single short thesis is supremely pertinent and almost equally perilous. The author of *Aggression in Youth* has succeeded admirably in establishing that pertinence in the relevance of his material, and at the same time has avoided the danger of seeking to provide too inclusive an answer to the problems raised. It is surely incontestable that youth is on the move, more quickly than in any comparable historical period, and towards hitherto unexplored territory. Moreover in this journey, or pilgrimage, this same youth is tending to express attitudes of aggressiveness which, though by no means peculiar to the young, appear to be especially characteristic.

This latest addition to the publications of "The Care and Welfare Library" can claim two most attractive qualities, which are by no means always apparent in the now voluminous library of argument and prescription about these two profoundly important issues. It is personal through and through—the besetting sin of abstractiveness is completely exorcised. It is most agreeably humble—the sinful pride of dogmatism is almost entirely absent.

Since the purpose of a foreword is to whet the appetite rather than to describe the menu, I will do little more than venture the comment that this is a treatise for beginners. It is moreover, calculated to convince even many of those who may come to this book under the misapprehension they are already fairly well versed in the moral, sexual, social, educational, emotional and family aspects of "youth and aggression," how ignorant in fact they are when these matters are approached in depth. This ignorance is widespread and it is therefore no valid criticism of Roy Ridgway that his work is a primer and not a last word.

A school doctor's view by Dr. Ronald Gibson which is appended to the main chapters leaves us as he says "with thoughts." This is the merit of the document as a whole. Those who take the trouble to search their own thoughts as they contemplate those of the author will probably, as I do, find certain observations more penetrating than others. They may well be animated by the optimistic realism which, while not minimising the danger and often the evils of youthful aggression, sees the future with confidence rather than cynicism. They may equally feel as they put the book down that two propositions are established. The first is that the individual and society are interdependent—the aggressive youth is largely the refraction if not the reflection of a particular kind of society. In a different and less violent social environment he will make a different and a more genial response. The second is that the absence of self respect is the root of aggressiveness and the opportunity of such real *amour propre* is the goal of any intelligent and civilized attempt to serve the best interests of youth and in fact the interests of the rest of us as well.

London, March 1973.

Preface

ONE of the most shocking things I heard anyone say during the war was when an officer, who was going to be ordained after the war, waved his cane at me, while I was in a hospital bed, and declared that he would have no compunction at all in castrating a German without an anaesthetic. He also suggested that all Germans should have their "trigger" fingers amputated. This was because I had said that I didn't believe the Germans were *all* wicked people, an unpopular thing to say at that time, not long after Dunkirk.

The other soldiers on the ward, who seemed quite ordinary decent men, agreed with the officer; they said they felt the same : the only good German was a dead one.

"I was at Dunkirk," said one of them. "It was difficult to get anywhere near the Jerries ... but when I saw a wounded Jerry I didn't think twice about sticking a bayonet into his guts."

I was a conscientious objector and had been sentenced by a court martial to three months' imprisonment with hard labour for refusing to put on my uniform. I didn't, however, serve that sentence : it was commuted to twenty-eight days' detention and I was then discharged from the Army because, as the discharge papers put it, I was "unlikely to become an efficient soldier."

I then joined the Friends Ambulance Unit and worked with the Free French in a mobile hospital in the front line in Italy and France. I chose to do this work; I was not *ordered* to. This was important to me; I refused to accept work (in the Non-Combatant Corps) which a tribunal offered me, as an alternative to an obligation I did not recognise : an "obligation" which would have involved me in killing my fellow men, which I could not reconcile with my Christian beliefs. "Can you imagine Christ in the cockpit of a bombing plane?" I asked that officer who waved his cane at me.

I am not concerned now about whether I was right or wrong and I am not trying to justify myself. We live in different times. But perhaps memories can teach us something.

I was a young man then, as confused and obstinate as any young man today. I was afraid of being called a coward; so I sought dangerous work. I used to say, quoting the author Olaf Stapledon who served with the Friends Ambulance Unit in the First World War, that I wanted to make some kind of protest against the common folly, whilst at the same time sharing in the common ordeal. Fine words—but what did they really mean? What I couldn't bear was being ostracized. That was my motive in seeking dangerous work. Morally speaking, I was a coward (i.e. in seeking approval I lacked the courage to be myself); but some said I was courageous. I was judged on what I did, not on why I behaved as I did.

I am telling this story because (1) I believe that if you could only see yourself as you really are you could learn a lot more about human behaviour than anything you can find in books; and (2) because I believe you cannot praise or blame anyone who is said to be "good" or "bad" unless you know *why* he behaves as he does in the circumstances in which he lives. What, in the depth and loneliness of his being, is he saying to himself? Is it something quite different from what he is saying to other people? How can you judge or help anyone unless you know him at his deepest level or unless you know about the conflicts that are going on within him all the time, which he may be afraid to reveal to anyone?

This is our difficulty in dealing with aggression in youth or, for that matter, aggression or violence of any kind in which every age group is involved.

Young people say that they want to be themselves, but are not allowed to because (they say) society is run by the old for the old and that there is a conspiracy against youth.

What I hope to show in this book is that the problems of youth cannot be divorced from the problems of society. The individual and society are inter-dependent. You cannot become a person except in your encounter with others—that is to say, with the community. Or to put it another way, a person can only be said to be unique if his uniqueness can find expression in his interactions with others. If his uniqueness is denied—i.e. he is not allowed to be himself—both the individual and the community will suffer; and there is bound to be violence. There is, however, some hope for the future when young people say, as so many of them do these days, that "it's because we love that we are rebellious."

I

Knowing Ourselves

MOST books on social problems do not seem to be written by *a person*. They are statistical, impersonal accounts which endeavour to be objective, whereas problems, particularly those concerning youth, can in my opinion only fully be understood subjectively.

For this reason I begin with some personal reminiscences which concern the problem of understanding. Central to this problem of understanding others is how well you know yourself. I must therefore start by exploring my *own* vulnerability before discussing others who are vulnerable; I must talk about myself, reveal myself, share my subjectivity with others—otherwise I, too, will merely be looking at youth's problems from the *outside*.

We cannot look at what is going on in the world in a completely detached way, because we are *in* the world, and part of the world, so that what we see must include *ourselves*. We are bound to see things in the light of our own experiences; our own past will influence our understanding. And this is what the conflict between the generations is mainly about. Somebody with a long adult past meets, or lives with, or works with somebody with hardly any adult past at all—and what happens? There is very little communication between them because there is a difference in their ages of some twenty or thirty years. Each has grown up with a different set of values. The old have become fixed in their ways. The young are much more flexible.

What makes things even more complicated is that neither may be able to understand his or her own past. How you see the past (your personal mythology) may distort the present.

I remember sitting outside our home near Birkenhead, when I was four years old. It was a hot day. I was rolling balls of warm tar in the palms of my hands, like an artist handling some exciting new material; and everything was hot. In between the paving stones the tar was soft and could be scooped out with the fingers—long stringy shreds of tar which I rolled into balls. But the picture this conjures up of a child sitting *alone* is not how a small four-year-old sees himself. In fact he does not see himself; he does not, in an adult way, differentiate between himself and the outer world.

As I sat on the pavement I was aware that behind me was the terraced house, the last in a row, where my family lived; opposite was the house where a bank manager and his son, Freddy, who was my age, lived—we used to dress up, I remember, in his back yard and act to an imaginary audience. At the end of the road trams went by, to and from Woodside Ferry in Birkenhead. To the end of the world and back. All these things—and the warm sun and clear sky—were merged in my consciousness. I had, as I think every child has, a glimpse of the *oneness* mystics talk about. All the things I saw were a part of me and I was a part of everything else, and time was endless. There was no preoccupation with "before" and "after," pining for what is not, as there is when we grow older. A child does not feel the passage of time as something that goes on outside himself. He feels only the immediacy of time: the duration of whatever he happens to be doing, mingled with impressions of effort and expectation. Childhood is lived in eternity; the scheme of time is only imposed on the child by adults with their knowledge of death.

Sigmund Freud, famous exponent of psychoanalysis, begins at the end—with the neurotic or psychotic adult—and so, I think, gives us a distorted picture of childhood. On the other hand, Krishnamurti—who has a particular appeal to the young today —talks about "what is." We do not, he says, see "what is." if we did, then we should see the universe. Denying "what is" is the origin of conflict, since the beauty of the universe is in "what is" and to live without effort with "what is" is virtue.

Memories of childhood are all like my example of rolling balls of hot tar. It is only when we start recalling our *adolescence* that we cannot be sure that it is not all mere invention.

Memories of adolescence are of one's struggle to become a real person—someone who exists for himself, with his own idea of himself, carrying out his own acts. We cannot do this when we are still dependent on our parents. We have to reject father if he goes on behaving as if he owned us.

A lot of conflict in adolescence results from just this need to reject parents in order to become yourself. Often, therefore, memories of father are not of a man but of a situation: a situation from which you were trying to free yourself. Your memories of him are mixed up with your own feelings of guilt and anxiety, resentments, frustrations, your goals and so on. You remember the things about him that were among the determining factors in the development of your own sense of identity. You remember interactions in the family situation, but not people very clearly—neither can you talk about them in a really objective way.

Penny

One day last year I learned something about one of the problems of youth, which I found coincided to a certain extent with my own experience as a young man, when my nineteen-year-old daughter, Penny, applied for a place as a foundation student at the Winchester College of Art. Before the interview she was worried about how she should dress. She was wearing tight blue slacks that were too short for her and a yellow smock. She was very unhappy about those blue slacks and decided in the end to change into black ones. I saw her looking in the mirror, but she wasn't looking at herself; she was trying to imagine how she would appear to the people who were going to interview her. She was looking at herself as men see her. Was she the kind of woman that men find desirable?

My wife and I met Penny at a cafe after the interview.

"I'll never go to another interview in my life," she said. "It was awful. I said all the wrong things."

"What sort of questions did they ask you?" I enquired.

"Oh, they asked me what I thought of the Russian Exhibition I saw the other day with the school," said Penny. "I told them I didn't like it—it was full of hate. Then they asked me what did I think Art was and I said I didn't know . . . it's how you feel. They said, 'Don't you think there's something to learn in Art as there is in English or History?' I said yes, but got confused. I was trying to say the right things, but I know what they wanted—*they wanted me to be myself.*"

"What did they think of your drawing?" asked my wife.

"Oh, that!" said Penny. "They just looked at it. Didn't make any comment. I don't think they liked me. Only one in four gets in."

"Never mind, Penny," my wife said, "it's all experience." But Penny went on worrying about the poor impression she had made at the interview.

I remembered how I sometimes felt when I was in my teens. I could not make myself understood and often I did not have any opinion at all. I was not courageous enough to say, "I haven't an opinion about that." Either I got confused or I would give somebody else's opinion as my own. I kept putting on an act and people would say to me, "Why don't you be yourself?" But how *can* you be yourself when you do not know who you are? Who is that person in the mirror? You see a dozen different faces to choose from.

You become a "thing" in the world of others because you are conditioned from early childhood to exteriorise yourself in this way. Jean-Paul Sartre, French novelist and philosopher, said of his childhood, "My true self, my character and my name were in the hands of adults. . . ." This was true of me and of most children. In the company of adults I saw myself only through the eyes of my parents and grandmother. Like Sartre, I was condemned to please. In the presence of others I was play-acting all the time. Wearing the fancy dress that was fashionable for children in the post-war years—a sailor suit, which bestowed on me the cultural identity of a great maritime nation—and scrubbed clean, I positively oozed charm and was forever smiling. My parents were proud of me, showed me off to friends and relations . . . "Look what a good boy Roy is. How happy he is. . . ."

I was a possession my parents were proud of—a "thing" like any piece of furniture around the house—the envy of others. To be a "thing," the object of envy or admiration, is not difficult for a child; but one feels an imposter as one grows older. Because one is constantly being required to live up to somebody else's ideas of what one should be one is, in effect, a part of that somebody else and one puts the same pressures on other people. The one thing you are not encouraged to do is to have any confidence in yourself and to be yourself.

One way of finding out if the "I" that I feel is my unique self really exists is by punching "you" on the nose. I then feel a real person, because you no longer treat me as an object in your world, but as someone whose behaviour is a threat to you and the only way you can restore the relationship of subject/object is by dealing me a much harder blow on my nose. But if you have not knocked me out, I will play dirty, and kick you hard on the shin or punch you in the stomach so that you double up and cannot, for a moment at least, hit back. If you prove to be physically stronger than I am, I can hurt you through one of your possessions which are a part of you. I can slash the tyres of your car, for instance. The only way to stop an escalation of hatred and aggression is for one of us to call a halt and stand back and try to see the other as a subject : to see the other as he is and to look for elements of justifiable motivation in the other's behaviour.

2

Individual Development

THE real difficulty in adolescence is self-control. How do you become the master of your soul? First of all you have to know who you are; but this was never discussed when I was a boy. Your identity was decided for you, first by your family, then by your school. The feeling of belonging to others made it difficult for you to feel a real person, and yet you must stand on your own feet. At one moment your independence was denied you, at the next you were blamed for not having a mind of your own.

The only book in my home on the subject of self-control was one called *The Human Machine*, which belonged to my father. It was written by E. R. Thompson and consisted of short articles reprinted from the magazine *John Bull*. There were articles on almost every human problem—a different problem and answer on every page. How to get up in the morning. . . . How to make money. . . . How to Concentrate. . . . Facing Fear. . . . How to acquire good habits. . . . Everything was cut and dried . . . problem, answer; problem, answer.

To be in control of oneself, one gathered, was mostly a matter of "will power." "Self-mastery," wrote Thompson, "involves an uphill fight every step of the way, a long fight in which victory can only be attained by patience, practice and perseverance." It worried me sometimes that I did not seem to possess much of the will power needed in the uphill fight. God evidently had forgotten to charge the batteries.

My father believed that success was an attitude of mind, that everyone was capable of "reaching the top." But we are not all born with equal abilities; some are more talented than others. And what his book did not tell me was this: supposing one were just an ordinary person, and did not have a high I.Q. and did not want to be a Milton or a Mozart, overcoming great physical disabilities as they did, what then? For me, a turning point came when I was eighteen and attended a lecture given in Liverpool by Dr. Alfred Adler, the Austrian psychiatrist.

Adler said that we had to change our whole attitude to children. We had to appraise them at their highest and not keep drawing attention to their faults. "Each child," said Adler, "is its own composer—it develops its own style—and if it is delinquent, what needs changing is not one single mistake, but the whole melody of its life. You can succeed only if the child understands more than you understand. You must change the manner it relates itself to life, the symptoms of lying, stealing and everything being forgotten."

Adler spoke of dangerous corners in a child's life.

/"When a child plays truant, breaks into shops, takes money, and so forth," he said, "you will probably find that some situation has arisen for which the child has not been prepared. Bad behaviour might be due to the birth of another child in the family, the death of a mother, the arrival of a stepmother, a new school, a change of teacher, the pampering of a child during a long illness, followed, when the child recovers, by strictness. Delinquency is always the result of some experience the child cannot assimilate. If it is an adolescent you are dealing with, the reason for his behaviour is that he has more possibilities and opportunities and wants to prove that he is grown up. Like everybody who wants to prove something, he is apt to go too far. There are so many dangerous corners one must know about. Why is the child unprepared? In what way have you failed to prepare him for the difficulties of life? In most cases the reasons for bad behaviour will be found in some physical imperfection, the parents' style of life or neglect."/

Adler was one of the first psychologists to investigate the child's situation in the family. He was able to show that the child's position as first, second or third child or as an only child had a profound effect on the way his character developed. But

Adler and his contemporaries, who had worked with Freud, were mainly concerned about the individual's problems and the mechanisms employed to deal with conflict and anxiety : e.g. Adler's theory of compensation or the conception of repression initially developed by Freud and the psychoanalysts.

Today we don't think of a person as someone living, as it were, in isolation from others. He has a family, and belongs to other groups, at school, university, in the factory or offices; and we cannot change his life style unless we can also change the style of his family life, the style of his education and ultimately the style of society. And we cannot change anything unless we have the co-operation of others about the need and methods of making changes.

One cannot control oneself or others as if it were only a matter of pushing a button to make the "will" function. "This is what I want . . . this is the way things will happen. This will happen according to how I want it to happen." But, of course, nothing ever happens in the way you want it to. The difficulty is in reconciling your own needs with those of others. The individual is only part of a system we call the family which in turn is part of a larger system we call society and the part can never control the whole.

Often, the situation in which you find yourself determines the sort of person you are. Your situation brands you as alien, unlovable, deviant; or it lays an accolade of respectability on your shoulder; it provides you with the clothes you wear, the language you speak; it creases your brow, brightens your eyes, gnarls your hands; it determines the way you walk or swagger, what you eat and drink and where you go for your holidays.

Illustrating the point about what has been called "situational determinism" I like the story of a policeman who watched a little boy running round a block of flats. After the boy had run past him on his way round the block for the twentieth time, the policeman finally asked him what he was doing. The boy said he was running away from home, but his father would not let him cross the road! In other words, the little boy was trapped in his situation.

In a foolish situation you are a fool. In the company of fools you will tend to adopt an attitude of pseudo-stupidity for fear of causing offence. Knowledge can humiliate. In a slum environment where most young people are delinquents you will, if you are young, be utterly miserable if you do not join the others and do what they do. They will call you "chicken." Where delinquency has the approval of your friends, who may form themselves into a gang that is committed to social warfare, and you are a timid person who is afraid to take part in their activities, you are the one who seems abnormal. And, in fact, you *are*. In a society of delinquents, it is normal to be a delinquent.

The sociologist and psychologist, J. H. Sprott, found two adjacent streets in Nottingham, one respectable, the other not. In the respectable street children were taught the "value of money," and parents took a grave view of stealing. In the other street money was easily come by and the children thought nothing of pinching. It boils down to this—it is hard to see yourself in your own situation, but if you can then you will know the solution to your problems. Move to "another street"—one of your own choosing where you have a chance to be yourself.

3

The Richmond Fellowship

A CHANCE to be themselves is what the Richmond Fellowship hostels offer to people who are disturbed in one way or another, largely because of feelings of insecurity or inadequacy engendered by conflicts or neglect or scapegoating in the family situation. They are people who are trying to get away from their situation, but find they cannot cross the road. The Richmond Fellowship helps them to do just that.

The hostels are therapeutic communities. Each house is a neighbourhood project—a co-operative effort—and provides a meeting place for the neighbourhood and those who have become alienated from their fellow men.

The founder, Miss Elly Jansen, maintains that it is insufficient merely to express concern for those identified as casualties in our society. "The whole issue of how we live in society," she says, "is an important one, and there are many people who will become casualties, or live an impoverished life, unless we take positive steps to prevent or reduce the destructive elements in society that impinge upon us all. We are daily confronted with disturbing events and forces perceived as destructive, such as labour disputes, student protests and race riots—but can we satisfy one group only at the expense of another? Does one group in reaching for health create conditions that produce mental illness in others?"

The way some people are being ground down by the destructive forces in our society and the way the Richmond Fellowship is trying to help them can best be explained in the words of a number of the young inmates of Lancaster House in London.

Jenifer

Nineteen-year-old Jenifer is an only child, the daughter of a doctor. "I always wanted brothers and sisters," she said, "and this has been one of my major frustrations in life.

"My mother was very young when she married—young looking, young behaving, sprightly, gay, jolly and full of confidence. Until I was about eleven I didn't have any emotional difficulties with her at all—but she seems to have been the real cause of my emotional difficulties in life because my father rarely saw me except at week-ends because he was always a very busy man.

"I often disagreed with my mother over attitudes of behaviour. She would expect me to be very polite and formal and she would do certain things that were thought well of by people of her generation but which I didn't think necessary when I was young. For instance, if we had a dinner party she'd always expect me to sit and talk to the guests before dinner, to have my meal with them, and to talk to them after and I remember I wasn't allowed to go to bed until quite late and this used to happen quite often and caused the resentment and annoyance that would build up.

"The same resentment built up in me over a lot of things. When we went out together she would insist that I should wear the things *she* wanted. If she didn't like my friends she didn't want *me* to like them . . . and also her friends—the friends that she liked, the old biddies, she wanted me to think the world of. And, if anything, it had the adverse effect on me. I just didn't want to associate with her friends at all. And I always found with my mother that instead of criticising me in a calm, constructive way, she would do it in a rather hysterical destructive manner. I remember she once told me I was as rotten as an apple right the way through, and I'm afraid I've never forgotten this. I was terribly upset about it.

25

"I suppose I must have been about eleven at the time, but I took it to heart—and a lot of other things I took to heart as well. She was a very highly-strung woman and she would get very emotional about things and I thought at one stage she was going through a mental breakdown.

"She was terribly frustrated with me because I wasn't doing well at school, and I wasn't making good relationships with people at school. Countless times I would come home saying, 'I've got no friends' or 'I'm very unpopular in the class, what am I going to do?' sort of thing, and try as my parents did, they couldn't find a solution and they suggested that I should see a local psychiatrist. I was against the idea and never did anything about it.

"Anyway, when I was twelve I went to boarding school in England and my relationships did not improve at all. I would come home for the holidays and for the first week or so I'd get on fine with my mother. She was so pleased to see me—but then we'd have our rows again—we'd get into tantrums. I'd go off and sulk. She'd go off and sulk. And we'd both end up hitting each other on the head.

"However, the situation got slightly better as time went on until I was sixteen. Then I came home one July to discover that my father had been living with another woman for about three months and that he was going to leave my mother and the house and everything—just completely abandon it. I just didn't know how to take this and got into terrible emotional knots about it. I became unpopular with the woman my father was going out with and I 'put my foot in it' with my mother the whole time. I really was totally useless to everyone."

Instead of asking what is wrong with Jenny, one should ask what is wrong with the family? To help Jenny a psychotherapist should get the whole family together and try to sort out what is happening to them, because it is not just Jenny who is sick, but the whole family.

The family situation is the most difficult to control. To achieve harmony in the family a balance has to be struck between individual creativity and collective activity. Each of us in the family situation has his or her own private battle, which is lost or won according to the support given by other members of the family. Take, for example, a family I know : Mrs. B., aged fifty, is a personnel manager, always very busy and at the moment the main provider (financially); Mr. B., who is fifty-five, is out of work; the eldest son, Arnold, is twenty-four, married and has two children; the daughter, Jane, who is nineteen, was backward at school, mainly because of her shyness, but is now beginning to edge ahead of her friends because she is always reading (which is no longer the escape it was in her early teens) and is learning to be a secretary at a Polytechnic; the youngest son, John, has asthma and is at boarding school.

Mr. B's battle concerns his age : he fears the approach of old age and is also afraid that he will not find another job at fifty-five unless he accepts some menial work. Mrs. B's problems are the imminent approach of the menopause and the loneliness she feels now that the family are growing up and no longer so dependent on her. Arnold's problem is that of a young man with a family he finds it difficult to support. Jane has her shyness to overcome—an identity problem. John finds it difficult to keep up with others, especially in strenuous outdoor activities, because of his physical disability.

A situation of this kind could lead to a lot of conflict within the family. Everybody's problem would be unendurable without the support of the others; but Mr. and Mrs. B. and their family are happy and united. The problem of each is diminished through the support given by the others. There is a feeling of emotional security; and each member of the family is interested in some kind of creative activity : painting, music and writing.

The individual derives his or her strength from the family sense of unity and the family is strengthened by the individual's feeling of uniqueness and self-fulfilment. One member who is disturbed or sick can affect the behaviour of the others and the cause of the sickness (or who exactly it is who is sick) is not always very obvious. The cause may go back for generations or it may be in the extended family—in the parents' relations—or it may be outside the family in pressures at work or school. There are probably many different causes. One cannot point to any one factor and say with certainty, "That's where the trouble lies."

It is usually much more complicated than that; and every diagnosis must be tentative. If one cannot help the family as a whole, one must do one's best for the individual whose life has gone wrong. One way to help the individual is by taking him or her away from the group that is disturbed into another group where there is more sharing of responsibilities and where conflicts are brought into the open and discussed with absolute frankness.

Another problem that has to be faced by the older generation is that though we may see the remedy, we are sometimes too set in our ways to do anything about it.

Ian

Ian is eighteen-years-old, has a Polish father, a brother and two sisters. This is how he told his tragic story :

"I haven't lived with my father for about three years now. My mother left him. When I was growing up all I can remember of him was when he used to beat me and beat my brother and sisters and used to spend most of his time in the betting shop and he used to bust up my mother a lot.

"Although I achieved a place at a grammar school I was chucked out when I was fifteen. I went to work and I got in with people who carried weapons. Then I started taking drugs and it escalated and I took more and more drugs to keep me the sort of person I wanted to be. Finally I went to hospital for treatment and was referred to Lancaster House by my social worker.

"When I was on the drugs, the people I was 'tripping' with seemed to be oppressing me, so I tried to keep away from them as much as possible. Then they started to oppress me more because they could see I was scared of them, and in the end I tried to kill them and they tried to kill me . . . I just felt I was going mad."

I asked Ian if he saw killing someone being an answer to his problem. He said he did because if he killed he would be imprisoned "and that would be an escape and I'd be locked up for thirty years and no one would have to come near me".

Alan, a sixteen-year-old, who has had a history of violence and trouble with the police and came to Lancaster House from an approved school, was asked how he felt about being locked up; Jenny, the middle-class girl whose story I have told also joined in the discussion; by accepting herself she could accept the others.

Alan: "I agree with Ian. I feel it's pretty true, because when I went inside I used to treat it as a sort of holiday, which it was in a sense. I went to Ardell, practically the most advanced approved school in the world, and you're pretty free—you're not forced to do anything. There's no bars, no locks or anything."

Ian: "Better than home, wasn't it?"

Alan: Yes, it was."

Ian: "My brother, when he was twelve, was put into Council care and when he was eighteen he was let out. If he wasn't a good boy, he'd be put back into care. It was a nice big house in nice big grounds but if he went home he'd have the choice of my screaming mother and my old man."

Alan: "I found that the more violent I was, the more friends I had. They were kind of scared of me. Not real friends; but I'd built up a reputation for violence and they respected me—not for what I was, but for what I could do.

"So I had my gang around me at the football match, and everywhere. There was only one thing wrong. If any of my mates was in a fight, it was not them wot got pulled in, it was me. I just got into more trouble all the time, started arguments with me parents and everything. Then me Dad started hitting me. So I turned round and hit him one and walked out—that was the last time he saw me till I was up at court."

"Do you know who you are?"

Alan: "This place has taught me roughly what I am, because I'm the only really violent person here—physically, you know. It's possible for me just to say something . . . Well, last night I said something and someone was in tears. You know, I do it mentally, physically and emotionally.

"I've destroyed people without even touching them . . . just keeping on at them, finding out what their weak spot is and then just playing on it all the time. I used to get enjoyment out of it. I've been hurt in the past, so why shouldn't other people get hurt now.

"I started doing what I wanted with people. I came to the stage where I actually shot a bloke a couple of times. It was just a fight. One of my mates had a gun. And this other bloke drew a knife on me, you know, so I just shot him. He happened to be an Arsenal supporter."

Steve

Like many other people suffering from a sense of extreme social isolation, Steve attempted suicide twice before he came to Lancaster House.

"For the first two years of my life," said Steve, "I was with my real Mum. My dad had run off. There were ten of us and my mum couldn't cope. So we were all distributed to children's homes."

Then Steve and his sister were adopted when he was eight and a half. His foster mother, he says, is extremely neurotic. "She used to push me round and that and I started getting pretty violent. I would kick my dad around and I hit my mum once. We had an argument about something and she started pulling my hair. . . . But I like my dad a lot. I think the world of him. There was a relationship between me and my dad deep down. But we just couldn't reach each other."

Steve became very aggressive in the home. He would smash windows and break down doors and his father had to call the police on several occasions. Finally a welfare officer called to discuss his problems and he was persuaded to leave home. He got a job and became attached to a girl. "It was a pretty badly matched relationship. Still, we liked each other." Then at seventeen, following the death of his girl friend, Steve became depressed and attempted suicide and was admitted to a mental hospital where he remained for six weeks. After his discharge he was unable to find work and attempted suicide again.

"Life seemed pointless," said Steve. "I couldn't see how I was going to get anywhere. I thought it's either mental hospital or the grave. I used to save the barbiturates up in hospital. I've got some now and I'm still thinking about suicide. But I admit things have started going better since I came here.

"You get the feeling of being wanted. When I came here I had a lot of trouble settling down. People thought I was something like 'Psycho'—you know, the film—and I used to just walk around by myself in the middle of the night, creeping round the house. They told me what they thought of me and gave me two weeks' notice. They said I had two weeks to change —or go! And I changed. From then on I got on very well in this community. I'm communicating from inside myself now instead of on the surface. My trouble was, I just missed out on childhood. I had the wrong sort of image of myself—of someone who wasn't wanted. All these years I've been living a lie. Now I know what's going on, which is not what I used to think was going on."

4

Growing Up

MOST of the young people at Lancaster House have experienced difficulty in making rewarding relationships.

"People come here," says Mike Pegg,* the warden, "with all sorts of labels—personality disorders, schizophrenia or whatever. I take no notice of the label. One certain way to get someone really screwed up is to call him a psychopath."

At Lancaster House they try to create time and space where youngsters can find out who they are and what they want to do in life. The young people try to get close to each other.

"You can call that involvement, or you can call it human contact," says Mike, "but I think the thing that helps a person most of all is that there's someone in his life who can make him feel important and special so that he feels he can say and do what he wants. 'I'm not going to be judged. The other person loves me in the sense of wanting things *for* me, not *from* me.' "

Involvement requires a lot from each person, especially from the sort of young people who come to Lancaster House who have, as Mike says, been "really screwed up" in their families. They have become extremely defensive and find it very difficult to talk honestly about themselves.

It is in talking about themselves to one another that they find the answers to the questions, "Who am I? What am I going to do with myself? How can I find fulfilment?"

"They can only find out who they are," says Mike, "if they

* Mike Pegg is twenty-six. He left school at fifteen and worked on a Rolls Royce assembly line. The monotony of the work "drove him mad" and he left to do social work. He joined the Richmond Fellowship, took his A-levels last year (1971) and is leaving shortly to go to University.

• •

are prepared to be frank about themselves to other people. So that means they have to feel safe—safe in order to be vulnerable. We have to create an atmosphere of safety here where people can say 'O.K. I'll open up and I don't mind if anybody clobbers me.' That's very difficult with people here—it's a big step for them to take—because all they've learnt in their families is that the only way to communicate is to hurt others—because they've been hurt themselves. That's the only pattern they know.

"And the only way to learn to become vulnerable is by having models—and, well, models start with me. If I'm not willing to share my confusion, if I'm not willing to cry or laugh in front of others, how the hell is anyone else going to learn how to do it?"

Then having got so far, where people can talk to one another openly and honestly, the next thing to learn is how to become a different person. This happens when people start *wanting* to be different.

"The way people grow is by saying, 'This is what I want. This is what I'm going to do.' People who come here feel terribly hopeless because at school, for example, they've often been told that they're useless—and so many of them have got a poor picture of schools. Also, in the family possibly they've had a mother or father who have been screaming at them. 'You're no good. You're no good. We'd be O.K. if it weren't for you. Your mother and I were all right before you came along. You're a mistake.' A person who has been treated like this is not going to think he's the nicest person in the world."

How do you help them to recover their self-respect?

"I personally believe," says Mike, "that people are basically very creative and positive, and if you like to use the terms, good and kind. They're out to help each other and they like to fulfil themselves in such a way that doesn't hurt other people. People should be allowed a chance to be accepted, to be told that they're worthwhile, that they're not failures, that they are in fact successes, that they have something unique to offer. Many of those who come here come for the specific reason that they've been told they're hopeless.

"So very often it's merely a question of people changing the direction of their energy. A guy called Carl Rogers said that the good life was not a destination, but a direction. For me, at least, it is a direction—trying to make people feel more themselves rather than less themselves."

Mike Pegg likes to think, as he put it, that he is "adding" to people rather than taking something away from them.

"There's a taboo on people asking the question 'What do I want?' What they should want is always being presented to them. It's what happens, for instance, in a self-service cafeteria— if you want cauliflower cheese, peas and potatoes, that's O.K. because it's on the menu, but if you want beans instead of peas, you've had it!

"However, when we ask people here what they want or how they want to live, they usually say simple things—they want to be married, they want good relationships and so on.

"The youngsters at Lancaster House have in the past put most of their energy in fact, into stopping themselves from getting the very things they want. A girl of sixteen or seventeen, for example, wants to be loved more than anything else, but what she might do is to frighten people off by yelling and shouting at them. So the simple answer to her problem is to put all her energy into loving people instead of hurting them—and then she will get what she wants. It is so very simple really—but not so simple for those who have never been loved in their families— who have had no models.

"One way to help people achieve their goals is by giving them enough time to unwind and get rid of all their tensions—all the muck that's inside them—all the anger they've got, all the dis- illusionment there. People who have grown up in the wrong way have to grow down before they can grow up again in the right way. Very often people who come here have spent their lives fighting others—fighting the family, the institution, father figures and so on. We give them very little to fight here. When they find themselves in this situation where there's nobody to fight because nobody's making them do anything, they might say to themselves, "Well, there's nobody left to punch—so what am I going to do with my life?"

At one time at Lancaster House they had very strict work rules; everybody was put to work at something and they were not allowed to slack. "That was O.K. The house was spotless, but I don't know what difference it was making to the people who were doing the work," said Mike Pegg. "They were only working because they wanted to stay here.

"I think work can be very helpful to people if that's what they choose to do, but they have to want to do it. When people come here now we no longer insist that they should work—and it might be six months before they do work. They sit around, lie in bed all day, if that's what they want, or play records."

To have time "to find yourself", to feel that the present is not being taken away from you for some hypothetical future happiness—jam tomorrow—is important.

/This time of waiting before a young person commits himself or herself to an adult role is called by Erik Erikson the "psychosocial moratorium." "It is," says this writer, "a delay of adult commitments, and yet it is not only a delay. It is a period characterised by a selective permissiveness on the part of society and of provocative playfulness on the part of youth. . . . Much of juvenile delinquency, especially in its organized form, must be considered to be an attempt at the creation of a psychosocial moratorium. During this period young people could be so easily crushed by being forced into a mould. "This," says Erikson, "we must consider carefully, for the label or diagnosis one acquires during the psychosocial moratorium is of the utmost importance for the process of identity formation."/

During this period a young man is often told that he is lazy, a "layabout," or lacks drive or motivation and this is undoubtedly the cause of a great deal of friction in the home and of some of the aggressive behaviour and hooliganism outside the home. But though the young person has no clear, definable goal, he feels his own uniqueness "that I am I and no one else". . . "no one is going to push me around."

He will infuriate his parents because he seems to be taking so long "to settle down." And at first he may start looking for answers in gang activity (if he comes from a poor environment) or involvement in political or social protest, or in religion, particularly nowadays in the religions of the East that teach passivity and detachment from worldly ambitions—non-involvement in an acquisitive society.

The moratorium, Erikson points out, is not necessarily consciously experienced. "On the contrary, the young individual may feel deeply committed and may learn only much later that what he took so seriously was only a period of transition; many 'recovered' delinquents probably feel quite estranged about the 'foolishness' that has passed." Some "end up in a social 'pocket' from which there is no return. Then the moratorium has failed; the individual is defined too early, and he has committed himself because circumstances or, indeed, authorities have committed him."

/ We should give our young people time to grow up. The "cure" for adolescence belongs to the passage of time and to the gradual maturation processes; these together do in the end result in the emergence of the adult person. /

In helping his young people Mike Pegg sits alongside them and then opposite them. They open up to him and he opens up to them. Nobody is "up" and nobody is "down." The kind of relationship they are seeking has been called an "I-Thou" relationship, as distinct from an "I-It" relationship which places people in categories—father, son; teacher, pupil; doctor, patient; and so on. There are those who are "up" and others who are "down." The "I-Thou" relationship, on the other hand, acknowledges the special, unique qualities of the other person that defy classification.

5

Aggression at Home

MEN are undoubtedly more aggressive than women and, apart from the violent-prone psychopath, a man in a group is capable of more violent behaviour than he is without the support of the group.

A man wears a different mask for different occasions. He puts on a different mask at work from the one he wears at home—and at home he is a different person when alone with his wife from the sort of person he is when his children or guests are present. As a member of a group his behaviour sometimes reverts to more primitive forms; he can become like an animal in a pack. Thus a fairly quiet boy at home may be capable of extremely aggressive behaviour in a gang when he puts on his animal mask. A mother of such a boy will often say, "I don't believe it. My Jack is not like that. It must be the others. . . ."

A whole area or town or city, where people are herded closely together (it is significant that we use the word "herd" in this way) can become violent. Liverpool, for example, has been described like this: "It is a strange town, it gets obsessed by everything it does. It is a town made up of different races, a city full of neighbourhoods, full of gangs and, outside Glasgow, the rawest, most passionate place in Britain.

"It has a certain black style of its own, a private strength and humour and awareness, real violence, and it is also grim, very much so. After the pubs close down everyone stands out on corners and watches what happens and has nowhere to go. Clubs are small, sweaty and dumb. Kids don't move by themselves or they get nutted by the guerrillas. This is America in England: a night out ends almost inevitably by a punch on the nose."

There are gangs in plenty of other towns than Liverpool, all with a strange "moral element" of their own. There are things one can and cannot do; and there is courage of a sort./Gangs are dynamic entities: cruel but dynamic, with a collective will and assertiveness—and this is just what attracts youngsters to them. Freud's explanation of the individual's behaviour in such a group is that it is the expression of the "ego ideal," a criticizing and observing element of the ego that is subject to conditioning. A person in love is often said to be blindly in love—he or she will do anything at all for the loved one, and in the same way a group will "blindly" follow its leader./

A reason for the behaviour of all-male groups can be found in the need of the male to assert his masculinity through what is known as the "bonding" process—i.e. getting together with other males in a competitive or aggressive way. Partly as a result of the sexual drive, for instance, gangs establish hierarchies in which the strongest, ablest and bravest become leaders, and weaklings and cowards are rejected by both males and females—"none but the bravest deserves the fair." Some girls, notably those from a poor environment, will admire the exploits of young hooligans in gangs; and for this reason the males are spurred on to commit acts of violence. It is a pity that it is usually one boy, and not his partners in crime, who appears before the magistrate.

It is not, however, thought that gangs in this country are a very serious menace and, according to some, may even serve a useful purpose in helping youngsters to discharge the emotional tensions of adolescence. Gang larking about is seen as being mainly concerned with "self-display and mutual support in the difficult business of extricating themselves from an uncomfortably close emotional dependence at home."

/There is a great deal of distortion, even fantasy or folklore, concerning adolescent violence and vandalism. Research on gangs shows that the dominant preoccupation of city gangs is not assault on persons or property, but theft. In an intensive two-year study of 700 members of twenty-one gangs (selected on the basis of their reputation for toughness) it was found that only

17 per cent of their offences involved an element of violence. And of 1,375 "aggressive acts" less than 7 per cent consisted of simple physical attack on persons and property. Mostly the acts involved were teasing, sarcasm and verbal derogation.

Another myth is the so-called "pointlessness" of the behaviour of gangs. Gang violence is usually described in the press as "senseless," "meaningless," "wanton" and so on, but research has shown that violence is directed and not "the wanton out-pouring of diffuse aggression." The cost and extent of violence in seaside resorts is also exaggerated.

It has always been true that young people have felt the need to get together with others of their own age group who have common interests or grievances. Mostly these groups are law-abiding; they are brought together by a common interest in sport or some hobby or creative activity such as cricket, football or travel and they congregate at youth clubs or in school or they meet in one another's homes.

Though the underlying motive is the same—to get together with like-minded youths of their own age—mobs such as Hell's Angels are usually drawn together by a common grievance against society, a feeling of being unwanted. They do not like the lives that have been invented for them so they start inventing their own. Often they are boys, says Mr Paul Willis, of the Centre for Contemporary Cultural Studies at Birmingham University, "whose opportunities are blocked by socio-economic conditions. They feel they can't get on in the middle class fashion. . . . So they operate an alternative set of values. Their notions of masculinity and recreation are different. They feel it more important to be able to handle oneself in a fight than to be able to play football well. Their values are blunter. They have working class attitudes, a rough bonhomie, a cheek and 'front' before authority."

Since the war we have had the Rockers, the Teds, the Greasers, the Mods, the Skinheads—every generation produces its young hooligans; the uniform changes, but the behaviour remains the same. They have a code of their own. They value

39

toughness and loyalty—qualities that could probably be put to good use in some more productive activity.

A member of a Birmingham gang described their ethic as follows: "Mob law says that if one stands, all must stand with him and fight, even if it's just a wild young lad. Mob law says ten kids don't go for one. That's a wanker's trick. [A wanker is any vicious cowardly fighter, anyone too weak or puny to fight, or simply a harmless outsider.] Society law says you're guilty because you've beaten someone up or killed them. Mob law says if this happens in a fair fight, you've done no wrong. Mob law says you don't grass on your mates, even if it will get you off a charge. Mob law says you *look after* your mates." The most menacing of all gangs in recent years are the Hell's Angels, an import from the U.S.A., who have as their motto "sex, sin and savagery." The fantasy or folklore is that they are prepared to maim or kill and beat up people. They do sometimes throw stones into shop windows and dash through towns at reckless speeds on their motorcycles; and there was a terrible case of gang rape for which a group of Hell's Angels were given long prison sentences at Winchester Assizes not so long ago. They also have their own marriage ceremony in which a motor-cycle manual is used instead of a Bible and the couple both have to swear that "the bike" comes before everything else.

"Buttons"—twenty-three-year-old Peter Welsh—is president of what he describes as the only Hell's Angels Chapter in England, chartered, he says, by the original San Francisco Hell's Angels. In his biography Buttons declares "We are prepared to kill, maim or break anyone who crosses us . . . Our sole responsibility is to ourselves. To get drunk, doped up, and ride hell bent and carefree as fast and recklessly as we desire down any highway however dangerous."

Much of this kind of talk is probably just bragging, promoting an image of toughness, and the truth is that violent or aggressive young delinquents are usually inadequate and rather pathetic personalities who need wise and careful handling—only in this way can one hope to rescue them from a criminal path.

One should not exaggerate the problem of teenage delinquency. Only a minority are a danger to society. No more than
2 to 3 per cent of the seventeen to eighteen age group appear in
court for indictable offences in any one year and only a small
proportion of these commit acts of personal violence. One of the
reasons why so much is heard about teenage delinquency is that
it is the young person, rather than the hardened professional
criminal, who appears most frequently in court. In London, for
instance, 65 per cent of all those caught for robbery in 1971
were between ten and twenty years old. The proportion of
professional criminals arrested is therefore not likely to be very
high.

The English judiciary system, says the Commissioner of the
Metropolitan Police, is "effective only for dealing with the compliant—the weak, the stupid, the illiterate and the spontaneous
wrongdoers who comprise the vast majority of cases. It is ineffec-
tive to an alarming and harmful extent in dealing with the non-
compliant—those who set out to break the law and are able, by
experience or through advice to exploit its weaknesses."

A young man is sometimes led into a life of crime by a pre-
mature diagnosis—by being labelled a criminal, which he may
even welcome in preference to having no identity at all. It is at
this stage, when he commits his first offence, that we have the
best chance of helping him to change his view of himself.

Crime is only one of many ways in which a young man can
overcome his feelings of frustration and self-doubt. Crime is only
the tip of the iceberg. There is a great deal of aggression
which is usually ignored because it is regarded as part of the
painful process of growing up. This is the aggression of rejection
—of avoiding reality by denying it. "You don't know what it is
to have problems. You'll know better when you grow up. Don't
worry me with your stupid talk. Why don't you grow up? Oh,
get lost, I'm busy. Why do you sit around moping? Why don't
you do something . . . anything . . . don't just sit there. . . ." All
this is rejection.

41

An example of aggression in the home is the disguised command in the questions a father asks his son :

Father: What do you want to do when you leave school?
Son: Don't know.
Father: Haven't you ever thought about it?
Son: No.
Father: Do you want to make money?
Son: Yes.
Father: Would you like to join the Army?
Son: No.
Father: Would you like to be a salesman?
Son: Maybe.

What the father is saying here, of course, is "Why the hell don't you make up your mind about what you're going to do with your life?" And what the son would really like to say is, "What's it got to do with you?" There is a lot of repressed aggression in an exchange of this kind in which question/command is met with the vague, indifferent answer.

These are some of the ways in which one can upset young people :

1. For many the fact that you are not young yourself—that you are over the age of, say, forty—is enough to irritate young people unless (a) you happen to be someone like Timothy Leary, Fidel Castro, Herbert Marcuse, Mao Tse Tung, Bertrand Russell, Dr. Benjamin Spock, Dr. Alex Comfort, Dr. R. D. Laing; or (b) you don't live a respectable life in a nine-to-five job (you're an impoverished artist or writer or philosopher disapproved of by the Establishment); or (c) you break the law on principle for some humanitarian or idealistic reason; or (d) you're a Buddhist or a member of some other Eastern sect or you talk about Gurdgieff or Kierkegaard or Sartre or Kropotkin.

2. One of the main irritations of the nineteen-year-old is the sixteen-year-old; and one of the main irritations of young

people in their twenties is the teenager. All young people, from adolescence to early manhood, are irritated by father figures—doctors, professors, Establishment clergy, politicians, policemen, or anyone in a position of authority who "puts down" the young; or they are irritated by people who because they are (a) richer, (b) older and (c) own a house, an expensive car and other status symbols, believe that this automatically gives them the right to tell young people how to run their lives.

We call this the "permissive society," but in fact there are more restrictions today than ever before—one has only to consider the increased restrictions (inevitable in any complex society) on such things as car-driving, building houses, schools, income-tax and so forth.

3. Preaching. Saying, "I wasn't allowed to do that when I was young." Talking incessantly about right and wrong. Young people are more impressed by example than precept. They usually have their own morality, but are unable to talk about it to their elders; but they will argue about morals endlessly with their friends, because they are indeed searching for an answer that really means something to them and is not merely a set of ready-made values. They should be encouraged to take part in intelligent discussions with other age groups, preferably outside the family. For young people to find answers of their own is a big problem. They must be made to feel responsible for the freedom they demand; but preaching and talking down never helps. Most important of all is that the young should live in an environment where there is no fear.

6

Aggression at School

SCHOOLMASTERS are understandably very concerned about the growing problem of violence in schools. The National Association of Schoolmasters, producing evidence of 3,200 cases of "uncontainable violence" in 415 schools, are demanding the right to expel persistently rebellious pupils not only from their own schools, but from the present system of State Education, and recommend the setting up of special schools, or, in the case of some violent pupils, tuition in the home.

At their conference in April, 1972 they passed a resolution expressing concern at "the rising tide of violence, vandalism and tension in schools" and urged local authorities to support teachers who expel pupils guilty of persistent offences.

They pleaded for support for teachers seeking "acceptable standards of discipline" and there was a large vote in favour of bringing back the cane. Only sixteen of 800 delegates voted against a resolution in support of the cane. "I believe the cane should be available to the teacher," said one delegate, "and the school delinquent should be aware of its existence."

Dr. Eric Briault, the Education Officer of the Inner London Education Authority, blames "the character of society itself" for making the task of teachers so difficult today. "In a comprehensive school which seeks to meet the needs of a complete cross-section of society," he said, "there are bound to be individuals who reflect the ills of society and suffer corresponding handicaps."

Mrs. Thatcher, Education Secretary, has been conducting a fact finding investigation into violence and other behaviour problems in schools, including indiscipline and truancy. At a meeting called by her in July, 1972 the National Union of Teachers put forward a four-point programme to minimise violence and truancy. The suggestions made were:

1. More social work in schools.
2. More special programmes of work for older pupils.
3. More support services, such as the provision of trained psychologists, to deal with difficult children.
4. Better school buildings.

In schools, as elsewhere, there must of course be rules, but it is important that the person who makes the rules is respected not merely for his "toughness" but because he is *morally* strong. In other words, his actions are dictated by an inner strength that recognises the need for moral guidelines. But however hard a teacher tries in school, his task is made difficult, if not impossible, if there are no convincing models in the home.

Many young people have told me that they like their parents to make rules even if the youngsters kick against them, and it is a common experience to find children who get into trouble—particularly girls—are generally those whose parents opt out by saying nothing. For an individual to acquire moral, ethical or philosophical perspective he must have more than one reference point (that is, a parent, a teacher or a friend) whom he respects. "Successful navigation," as one headmaster put it, "requires more than one fix."

One cannot separate violence in schools from violence in society—much of which stems from adult uncertainty about right and wrong. Undoubtedly many young people are exploiting the confusion of the older generation. The problem of youth is therefore mainly a problem of the inadequacies of the older generation, a problem which is rarely discussed except by the young themselves.

The American Psychiatrist Bettelheim believes that we have been spoiling our children because we are "unwilling to risk displeasure from the child by imposing controls," a tendency which has perhaps been strengthened by a misinterpretation of

Freud's teaching to suggest that repression is wrong. Lacking a true justification for punishment, we coerce and yield erratically, as *our* convenience, not the need of the child, dictates. The child learns that punishment is inconsistent and vindictive, and intuitively senses our guilt and indecision. Unwittingly, we teach him that we can be bullied and he goes through life thinking that everyone else can be pushed around too.

When and how to say "Yes" and "No" is the main problem in exercising discipline. When a person is too demanding there is the temptation to say "No" to every request. And often the effect of saying "No" is spoilt by explanations, which is said to be mainly a middle-class habit. An example of such an explanation is "I don't know how you can ask me after all I have done for you." This kind of explanation suggests that with further argument the "No" may become "Yes". It is usually easier to say "Yes" than "No" and in our permissive society there are too many people saying "Yes" to everything.

There is some evidence that one of the causes of our moral uncertainty today arises from the rapid developments in technology changing our social structures and habits of living. Young people often complain of a loss of any sense of common purpose, and their moral sensitivity is shocked by the contrast between the intense effort devoted by their elders to the pursuit of material advantages, and the expenditure on military power, and their lack of concern for the suffering and under-nourished majority of mankind outside the industrial world.

It is suggested that what appears as a widespread rebellion of youth against authority is largely born of frustration caused by the absence of authority—in the sense of a lack not of severity, but of convinced and therefore convincing models of conduct.

What the schoolmasters are proposing is "more severity"—bring back the cane and so forth. One can, of course, sympathise with them, and the solution they propose may make their lives a lot easier : but it is the child who must be our main concern. It is, as everyone agrees, extremely difficult for teachers to control large classes without recourse to some form of punishment, some times harsh; but the problem is much more complex than the way it is sometimes presented.

One should not overlook the fact that there are various forms of delinquency, each calling for a different form of treatment, and recent legislation also recognises a wide range of behaviour as indicating psychological disorders that need *treatment* rather than punishment. Persistent truancy and staying out late at night are examples of such behaviour.

There are even schools themselves that, like families, streets or neighbourhoods, have taken on the character of delinquent communities and one can understand the motives behind current childrens' agitation for better conditions in schools. Those who conduct these campaigns argue that education is aimed at preparing children for adult roles, but when children take it upon themselves to behave in an adult way by pressing for better conditions in schools they are told that they have no rights.

One solution to the problem of children's demonstrations which some schools have adopted, is the formation of democratically-elected groups who can mediate between children and staff and can put forward suggestions for improvements in the running of schools. This is useful training in the way democracy works. There should also be a place in the school curriculum for moral, sociological and psychological studies; and children should be encouraged to do social work. A closer integration of school and neighbourhood should be encouraged.

Another body of opinion believes that modern teaching methods encourage violence in schools, and there are teachers who say that "progressive" ideas are undermining their authority.

So-called "progressive" schools, however, usually have a better record of non-violence than schools where traditional methods of teaching are still favoured. Sir Alec Clegg, education officer of the West Riding, mentioned in an article in *The Times* a good example of a progressive school which he visited. It was a junior school of 500 pupils, over 80 per cent of them sons and daughters of miners. "It was a dull building," he wrote, "but a forward looking school working entirely in new and informal ways; ways

47

which by some have been blamed for recent increases in juvenile delinquency. 'Have you had any youngsters before the court?' I asked. 'None for the last five years,' replied the head. On the same day I put the same question to two other heads working in similar schools and received a similar reply."

There have been tremendous improvements in education in junior schools in recent years and Sir Alec Clegg believes that the reason why they are on the whole happier places than secondary schools is that in the former children from their earliest years initiate and assume responsibility for much of their own learning, guided by and in collaboration with an observant teacher, whereas in the secondary school "the initiative and responsibility in which the junior school pupils thrive have to be reduced and the pupils told, albeit indirectly, 'This is what you have to do, this is how you do it. Do it and I will mark you and grade you accordingly.' " The quick learner who needs less help is usually treated as more important and more deserving than the slow who needs more.

Large classes and understaffing are often blamed for unruly behaviour in schools, but my own view is that at the root of the problem is the teaching of what I and many young people today believe to be the wrong values, which is not the fault of teachers themselves, but of our educational system. What we teach our children, or how we teach them depends largely on what we consider to be the main purpose of education. Is it to make children conform to the rules of a highly competitive society in which rivalry is encouraged or to give them a feeling of self-fulfilment, a sense of purpose in which they can feel themselves fully committed and involved?

Our educational system is mainly designed to train future employees rather than to develop future citizens. There is too much comparing of one child with another. Children are taught that to be good is to be *as good as* someone else or to be clever is to be *better than* someone else. They are often made to feel— by parents and teachers alike—that there is something shameful about failure. They are rarely allowed simply to be themselves.

There is too much training for exams in secondary schools and not enough training for life; too much emphasis on competition and individual achievement to the detriment of collaboration and teamwork; too much emphasis on future rewards and not enough emphasis on living now—which means living subjectively in the existential present where there is no separation between you and the world you live in.

Children come to school from different backgrounds—from homes where they may be bullied or ill-treated or neglected, or from homes where they may be pampered and where there are no rules, and also from homes where there is a real sense of family unity, emotional stability and the encouragement to be creative. Some parents place a high value on physical prowess or skill with the hands, others on intellectual pursuits; a child's style of life is fashioned in the home. But all these children from different backgrounds may be brought together in one classroom where the ability to pass exams is considered more important than almost anything else.

In primary schools the importance of play in the learning situation and in character building is nowadays generally recognised; but in secondary schools it is still more important to learn facts, even in subjects such as English Literature and History where there can be no real understanding unless there is understanding of the emotional content; and in these subjects a child whose sensibilities have not been allowed to develop will learn nothing useful though he may still possess the retentive memory necessary to pass exams.

I am no expert, but is seems to me that what is needed in our schools is what I would call "emotional streaming." Children from poor backgrounds, where there has been neglect or cruelty, should be separated from, say, children from intelligent homes where there are good relationships and emotional security. The former need more encouragement to develop qualities of courage, freedom, spontaneity and self-acceptance; and the others need encouragement to use their talents without being held back by the less talented.

49

The Government White Paper published in December, 1972 is a step in the right direction, particularly in its generous provision of Nursery Schools over the next ten years, to diminish social deprivation. Many children who stay at home during the most important first five years start school with a disadvantage which may affect them for the rest of their lives. Also the plans announced in the White Paper to expand the teacher force and to improve its quality, to reduce the average size of classes and to spend more money on school buildings will be welcomed by many. What one can't legislate for is moral standards; and it is in this area—where courage can achieve more than money—that there has to be more vigilance and soul-searching. I am sure—and hope—that Mrs. Thatcher's plans will undergo considerable modification over the next few years with the growing awareness of the need to help children to live *now* and not to be always projecting them into the future.

7

"Getting My Own Way"

IT largely depends on the way children are taught today to use their feelings of aggression that will determine what kind of world they will help to shape tomorrow.

The aggressive drive, which has a positive function in creating order in society, also constitutes a threat to man's survival, and the problem today is how to contain the surplus aggression which society generates.

The observations that follow are written by thirteen-year-olds at Leighton Park, a Quaker public school where the aim is to see that children are not ashamed of their own aggressive feelings but can use them in constructive ways.

AGGRESSION TEST

An interesting thing about aggression is that you do not know about your own until you take an aggression test. This does not mean hitting a test-your-strength machine or anything of that kind. It simply means sitting down and answering some questions.

The questions are somewhat mixed, ranging from everyday situations to impossibilities. The most impossible thing, however, is the final result. The people in charge of the test insinuate that my mildness is a cloak for destructive tendencies. Yes, they say that I am destructive—imagine it, *me* destructive! After that I felt like taking an anvil and smashing the test compilers over the head with it.

N. Woolford

AN AWFUL PERSON TO LIVE WITH

Aggression is a thing which overtakes us all from one time to another. Some of us are weak tempered people, some normal, some extremely bad tempered.

My temper is meant to be normal, but I am afraid that when I do not get my own way I have a tendency of becoming stubborn and extremely ill-tempered—I should think I am an awful person to live with . . . I have a bad habit of going and looking at something and then going into a trance, and then when my mother calls I just don't hear her.

I will not have people hurting animals. To bully an animal I think is absolutely insane. I disagree with those who say that because an animal is not a human it does not matter what you

51

do with it. Once I was forced to watch a boy washing his pen out in a jam jar of pond water with a minnow in it and then putting the dead body in someone else's inkpot. (Incidentally, because the ink smelt after two weeks, it was given to the head-master when next he wanted some ink.)

I do not mind animals being killed for science.

J. D. Pratt

WHITE V. BLACK

I was in a cafe when an old African man came in, followed by a fat English housewife. As the old man was asking for some tea, the waitress turned round and served the white woman; the man had to wait some time before they had finished their chat. This made me feel furious and aggressive. I felt like shouting out and pushing the waitress over on the ground.

Anthony Ridgway

TAKE RUGGER...

In a small society such as a school there are people who always spoil things for others. Take, for example, Rugger. There are three types of Rugger player—(a) the good Rugger player who plays a good clean game; (b) the aggressive Rugger player; and (c) the hater of Rugger. A encourages C and tells him that Rugger isn't as bad as all that, but during the game B comes along and thumps C when he hasn't got the ball. Poor C gets very discouraged and goes back to hating Rugger.

M. J. Turner

A GOOD OR BAD THING

Aggression is bad, when people become aggressive about the most trivial things, but I think it is a good thing for people to become aggressive about important things like stealing and cruelty.

I find myself that I only become aggressive when I can't stop somebody doing something I consider wrong. But before I become really cross, and in some cases resort to violence, I always try and persuade the other person not to do wrong. I suspect that aggression is an instinct, and however hard one tries, aggression will always come out in some form or another. For instance, it comes out as shouting at a fellow passenger on a bus, or cursing the motor mower because it won't work.

I think that aggression is a kind or release valve, therefore we could not live without it.

Huy W. Sperryn

AGGRESSION IS USELESS

I am not too aggressive, but according to a test in the *Sunday Times,* I am; this is nothing to go by.

Some types of aggression are useless and destructive, such as slashing train seats and smashing mirrors. Some types are not destructive. If you have your own way on a matter and your view is correct, then it is constructive. One can be aggressive about any trivial matter, such as arguing about a pencil or a missing games shirt. Aggression is usually useless at getting things done. One often sees it in the blowing of horns in a traffic jam or swearing at a light bulb that won't go in its socket.

G. Nash

NOT AGGRESSIVE, BUT...

I am not aggressive, but enjoy having my own way. Even if I do not outwardly show my anger over something, I really am thinking the opposite of what I am saying. For instance, if someone in a crowd treads on my foot and apologises, I say "Oh, that's all right," but inwardly curse him. Fortunately I can control my temper. If a restaurant service is poor, I do not create a scene, but make a note never to go there again. I am aggressive over some things. I am easily irritated and may fight the person who is irritating me. Usually the fight is a good thing and we end up shaking hands. I will quarrel if I am done out of anything but usually blame myself. Life is forever blaming something.

John Smith

ANGRY

You feel as if you could jump on them,
As if to kill them in anger,
It feels as if you had the strength
Of a hundred men.
You get in a kind of trance,
And go pushing people about,
The slightest thing that goes wrong
Makes you blame it on someone else.
If a person gets angry with you,
You try not to listen.

John Donald Williams, aged 11

(An award winning entry from the fifth *Daily Mirror* Children's Literary Competition.)

8

On Blaming Television

TELEVISION and newspapers are often blamed for the aggressive behaviour of young children today, but among those who are studying the problem there is a lot of controversy. It has been said by one social scientist that children nowadays fail to see the evil in horror and the wrong in violence and that they have lost their natural sympathy for the suffering of others. The trouble, it is said, is not that they are frightened by all the violence they see on television, but that they do *not* get frightened.

In a study of violence on American television, it was found that three major television networks put out programmes in a single week that showed a total of 113 shootings, 92 stabbings, 168 beatings, 9 stranglings and 179 other acts of violence. In the average American home the television is on more than six hours a day. Every fourteen minutes, on an average, there is a violent incident and every three quarters of an hour a killing. The average American between his second and sixty-fourth year spends 3,000 twenty-four hour days—almost nine years of his life—watching television and being "present" at 300,000 violent incidents and 100,000 killings.

There are those who say that violence in television drama has a cathartic effect, draining away pent-up hostile feelings in the viewer, but certainly as far as America is concerned this view is not entirely supported by the evidence available. Two American psychologists, Dr. Robert H. Liebert and Dr. Robert A. Baron, in a report to the American Psychological Association Convention, said that sixteen out of eighteen experimental studies

55

showed that viewing aggression can instigate subsequent aggression by the viewer.

An American senator, Thomas Dodd of Connecticut, chairman of a U.S. Senate sub-committee set up to investigate crime-sex-and-violence on television states :

"Glued to the T.V. set from the time they can walk, our children are getting an intensive training in all phases of crime from the ever-increasing array of Westerns and crime-detective programmes available to them. The past decade has seen T.V. come of age—it has also seen a 200 per cent increase in violence and delinquency."

Not only overseas, but in this country too, television production companies compete with one another in the amount of violence they can cram into their programmes and in dreaming up original slants in the way they present violence. Consider, for example, this advice given by a producer of *The Untouchables* to a member of his staff : "On page 31 of this script, I wish we could come up with a different device than running the man down with a car, as we have done this now in three different shows. I like the idea of the sadism, but I hope we can come up with another approach to it."

The reason given by the television companies for all this concentration on violence is that films that are full of horror and violence are bigger money spinners than straight forward drama in which there is no violence. Nevertheless, thoughtful people in the industry are showing increasing concern over the amount of violence shown in programmes to which children may be exposed and producers throughout the world are trying to draw up an international code that will classify films according to different age groups. The code will take into account the amount of violence in a programme, its dialogue and plot, background and general suitability.

There are countries, including France and Germany, that have a system by which parents can identify programmes that are considered unsuitable for children. British producers, however, have said that such a system is difficult to operate, and it has also been said that warnings about the violent nature of a programme may even encourage some children to watch more closely. It must also be acknowledged that in this country those programmes made specifically for children are of a very high quality.

In Britain some support for the view that violence on television encourages violent forms of behaviour was provided by Dr. Eron, Research Officer, Centre for Mass Communication Research at Leicester University. He reported having found a significant positive relationship between violence ratings of favourite television programmes, as reported by mothers and fathers, and aggressive behaviour of boys as rated at school. But nothing seems to have been said about the aggressive behaviour of parents; conceivably parental attitudes may have been largely to blame. Did the parents themselves watch the same violent programmes? This question wasn't asked.

There is probably as yet insufficient evidence in this country to show that delinquency can be explained in terms of the imitation of television models, although there is little doubt that some young children (and a few older ones) will inevitably confuse the rules of the real world and transfer television situations to real life. It has been found that delinquent boys use television more for excitement and less for relaxation, identifying themselves with violent characters, and are not so critical of programmes as non-delinquent boys. Their viewing is therefore a part of the pattern of their delinquency.

Thus a case can be made out for the need to concentrate mass communication research on what people do with the media than on what the media does to people. Of prime importance is the viewer's own values; what he brings to television will in no small measure determine what television does to or for him.

To blame television or films for the behaviour of people who translate fantasy into reality is really as absurd as blaming a match for starting a fire. We can only understand this problem subjectively. Some presentations of violence on television and films and in literature can illuminate dark areas of experience we are not aware of, but the effect is very diverse and different people react in different ways. Good parental attitudes and environment have more influence on the growing youngster than does television.

It is worth remembering in this connection that before the days of films, television and a popular press, there was much violence among those whose childhood was spent in a poor environment such as the East End of London where, even as recently as Edwardian times, thugs would kill for half a sovereign.

Some of the present concern about violence in youth arises through press methods of reporting—for instance the reporting of the same incident twice as if it were two separate incidents; the reporting of non-events ("Fears when Ton-up Boys Walk in Groundless", or "No Violence in Brighton Today"); interviews with gang leaders ("Why I Threw That Hammer" by "Mick the Wild One"). Folk villains and devils are paraded before us as if they were leading actors in a play.

Finally, in considering the effect of violence on film or in the printed word, one must accept the fact that many ordinary, non-violent people enjoy violence in films, books and newspapers. These people enjoy stories of horror and violence without in any way being affected by them, and probably this is true of the great majority of viewers and readers of horror tales. The world's literature, as studied at school, contains plenty of violence : *Macbeth, Julius Caesar, Oedipus Rex,* some of the novels of Dickens and Dostoevsky's *Crime and Punishment* to name but a few examples.

My daughter, Penny, found pleasure in reading a book about the cruelties of the Roman games in which there were lurid descriptions of how people were torn to pieces by lions and tigers—and of how on one occasion slaves were covered in oil and set alight to illuminate the arena. Penny said the book was "terrible," but nevertheless she couldn't put it down. And yet she is the kindest, most sensitive person and was once in tears when she found a squirrel caught in a trap. There is much that is baffling about human nature.

9

Emotional Knowledge

"EMOTIONAL knowledge" is essential if we are to understand people, especially young people who are disturbed in some way. You can learn about people from books—this is factual knowledge—but there is a world of difference between this kind of knowledge and emotional knowledge which is gained through "lived" experience.

In this chapter I want to deal with 1. the feelings behind words; 2. what one learns from the emotions; and 3. the importance of admitting to yourself and others that you have feelings which you may sometimes feel ashamed or embarrassed about. I am thinking particularly of young people, so the advice given here is mainly intended for them.

Much of what I have to say is dealt with in greater detail in three most important books: 1. *The Transparent Self* by Sidney Jourard; 2. *On Becoming a Person* by Carl Rogers; and 3. *Towards a Psychology of Being* by Abraham Maslow. All these books are about the psychology of health and are written for the layman, so they are not difficult to read: and I would recommend them to anyone interested in the problems of youth.

What these books have done for me is to help me to accept myself as I am (to be honest I should say that sometimes I can do this; not always) and because of this simple fact I have found that I am beginning to see things much more clearly—that is to say, I have a clearer understanding not only of my own feelings but of the feelings of others—sometimes! This knowledge is available to everyone: it merely means being absolutely honest about yourself. That is the important, and for many, very difficult first step. For you—unlike me—the "sometimes" can be "always". That is what I hope for young people.

But first, let me say something about words and their meanings: i.e. the things we say which don't always accurately describe our feelings. People sometimes use the wrong words or say one thing when they mean the exact opposite. An adolescent girl, for example, may say to her young man "I hate you" when she really means "I love you;" or she may say "No" when she desperately wants to say "Yes" or "Yes" when she feels she ought to say "No." That word "ought" is significant. What does it mean? It means, of course, that social pressures prevent the girl from saying what she really feels: "ought" comes between her and her feelings.

Most of us in our everyday dealings with one another communicate by employing socially accepted forms of speech—we are "grateful for . . . indebted to . . . appreciative of," and also we are "hurt (though not literally) or "sorry" or "ashamed to say." We use these words without thinking; we may not really be sorry for something we have done, but we all recognise the need to say so, because these polite forms of speech are designed to inhibit aggression between people. And this also applies sometimes to a gesture or to what is called a non-verbal signal, such as a smile or frown—the smile may be, as we say, "disarming," the frown is a threat, but cannot actually hurt; it is meant as a deterrent. The hand, which becomes a fist in combat is seen (by the animal that lurks in all of us) as a potential threat to others and at some stage in our social evolution it was immobilised in the handshake or in the way the hand is raised with the palm exposed in friendly greeting or in waving good-bye. We have our body language and our verbal language. For instance, you can tell the personality of a young man as he stands slouching at a street corner: we know what he is thinking before he says anything.

In recent years, through the work of ethologists, we have learnt a lot about ritualistic behaviour which has been developed over many thousands of years of evolution. Much of it goes back to our animal ancestry. Such ritualistic behaviour is absolutely essential if we are to avoid conflict with others. Without our rituals, including what we call good manners, human society would be intolerable. The polite words we use, which so many young people are now abandoning because they say they are unnecessary, are mostly ritualistic—which is not to deny their importance. (The young are right, of course, in the sense that in a perfect world rituals would be unnecessary; but ours is not a perfect world.)

Behind the polite things we say there may be quite different feelings. That old so-and-so who has just died . . . we didn't like him very much, and yet we may write "In fondest memory" or similar words on the card attached to the wreath we send for his funeral. This is mainly out of sympathy for the family of the bereaved.

All this has relevance to the problem of aggression among young people. "Why be polite?" they say. "Isn't it better to be honest than polite?" To which I would answer, "Yes and no," for reasons which I will give in a moment. But it's misunderstandings of this kind (about what words mean) that create conflict : what young people may see as honesty older people see as rudeness.

One can think of many examples of behaviour that is aimed at mitigating rather than intensifying the pain people feel on certain occasions. For instance, we don't go around being brutally frank to everyone we dislike. We are usually polite and tactful.

Forms of speech change, but the need for politeness remains. There are degrees of politeness and impoliteness and there are occasions when politeness is "off-putting." Take, for example, the simple request or command to close a door. This can be expressed in different ways :

Would you be good enough to close the door?—Question/ command used by an elderly person (hardly ever a young person) or by someone in authority, "putting down" a subordinate. Could be a rebuke or polite request.

Please close the door (rebuke) or Close the door, please (polite request).

Close the door (command) or *Close* the door (plea). Inflection can alter meaning.

Door!—Could be just a friendly rebuke: e.g. young person to a friend; schoolmaster to pupil. But never pupil to master or young person to an older person: then it would be impolite and aggressive.

No words at all—a glance can say a lot.

You can see from this how words can change their meanings how they have different meanings for different people and how important a tone of voice or gesture is. All this has to be learnt in the process of growing up.

Being polite is second nature to most adults; but adolescents are often embarrassed by simple things like not knowing how to start a conversation or how to put people at their ease, and their lack of experience in the niceties of social behaviour is also often seen as rudeness. This too—the gaucherie of youth—is a common cause of friction between parents and their children.

Another cause of friction is because of the pace at which we live today, our speech is often hurried and imprecise; and many of our reactions are born out of frustration and irritation because we can't do things more leisurely or because we simply haven't the time to think. We talk in unfinished sentences, relying on gestures or on the other person's familiarity with a subject to convey meaning. All this adolescents may find difficult to understand and consequently they often feel excluded from the conversation of older people. Especially are they puzzled by some of the value words (the do's and don'ts) that belong to the past. "Why?" they keep asking. "Why? Why? Why?" "Well, because it's simply not done" or "That's the way it is." And again there's really no time to explain: there's a train to catch, a meal to cook and so on. "Sorry, I can't stop to explain. Work it out for yourself . . ."

Words are the currency of love and friendship, but, as with

the awkward adolescent who is always saying the wrong thing—
but equally with the person who is always over-polite—they can
create barriers between people. You must always listen for
unspoken words, particularly when dealing with young people.
You must listen with the heart as well as the head and with the
eyes as well as the ears. Sometimes a gesture or facial expression
carries a much more potent message than the words spoken. A
very wise doctor, the late Michael Balint, who treated the whole
man and not just the symptoms of his illness, once said that to
understand others you must cultivate what he called "a calculated ability to listen."

There are, broadly speaking, two ways of listening—with
diffuse or wandering attention and with concentrated attention
and there are times when you can't avoid listening—people
force you to listen. In helping young people in trouble there
should always be concentrated attention and you should not
place yourself in a position where you are an unwilling listener.
You should always *choose* to listen. If you have other problems
on your mind, it is better to say to a young person who asks for
your advice, "Can we talk about this another time?"—but don't
be vague about it : suggest a precise time.

The way we listen is very important; but it is also important
to encourage young people to tell the truth about themselves.
They are, in fact, better at being frank than older people, but
they are not often given much encouragement to open up. If
you go on insisting that they must always be polite and respect-
ful, you will not get them to disclose very much about themselves.
There is a lot of aggression in the person who is always using
polite words. He is really hiding behind them, and because of
this it is difficult to get to know him or her.

To understand the other person you must know his "self,"
that is, his *experiencing* self, the way he experiences the world,
not the way he promotes himself, and not other people's "idea"
of the sort of person he is. If his "self" never comes through
to you—if he can't trust his own feelings—he must be very
unhappy and possibly mentally sick. There is, as Carl Rogers

63

and the other authors mentioned at the beginning of this chapter have shown, a connection between the amount of information a person is willing to disclose about himself and his general state of health. Hospital patients, for instance, by talking honestly about themselves have a better chance to get well than those who lie in bed saying nothing or very little to anyone. The same is true of disturbed adolescents.

I am not advocating, as many do these days, the closing of distances for the sake of a temporary contact, which is what happens in the encounter groups that are springing up everywhere these days. This can be a shock, especially for a young person. Deliberately creating a stress situation will break a person's defences and may shatter that person altogether. Keeping one's distance is necessary on occasions, but the adolescent who is afraid to reveal himself, even in the intimacy of his own family circle, is in need of help. He should feel safe enough to talk honestly about himself. Only in this way can he come to understand himself and can he grow. As Maslow says, we can't *force* a person to grow, we can only *coax* him to . . . "We must offer and not *force* . . . we must be quite ready not only to beckon forward, but to respect retreat to lick wounds, to recover strength." Young people must occasionally be left alone to try to resolve their own conflicts.

To be full of unresolved conflicts is numbing. Young people will just sit around because they are full of conflict. They are quite unable to make decisions—so they just do nothing. They will say they feel tired or will remain silent. At such a time they will reject any advice you care to give them; so that the answer to their problems is probably activity in which their emotions come into full play. But they should not be goaded into activity; they should be offered something interesting to do : not *forced* to do anything.

To make moral judgments, such as accusing a young person of lack of will power or laziness or spinelessness, can also do a great deal of harm. Take the case of Arnold, another of the young people I talked to at Lancaster House. Arnold, who is nineteen, has been in three mental hospitals and says his trouble was "ritualistic behaviour" and "psychosis." His sickness seems to have been caused by parental attitudes or, more precisely, by the ambiguous attitudes of parents who although they pampered him had an over-strict moral code. Also at school he was regarded as a "cissy" because he was more interested in books than sport.

"At school," he said, "I was picked on because I came from Hampstead and I like poetry and things like that, whereas the other boys liked football. I was always very tense in the family. I was very dependent on my parents and they played up to it. I knew that to get their attention all I had to do was to play sick.

"I used to take drugs. When I was sixteen I was disgusted with my body. I just felt it was a dirty thing that shouldn't ever be talked about... My parents probably had a lot to do with it... One day I was always wanting to wash myself; it became very bad, I couldn't stop it. My parents wondered what was the matter and sent me to a Child Guidance Clinic.

"It's only since I've been here at Lancaster House that I've discovered what is the matter. When I feel good inside I don't want to wash so much. I used to try to avoid touching things that would make me dirty."

Arnold was cured because he felt secure enough to talk about himself at Lancaster House: no one accused him of moral weakness or of being a "cissy". He could then open up—tell the truth about himself and not feel ashamed of his emotions.

A young person who has difficulty in making friends or is always in trouble with his teachers, his parents or others in authority should ask himself, "Who knows me?" If he asks members of his family and his classmates or workmates to tell him what they know about him, he will probably find the answers are diverse and that he hardly recognises the person they are describing. The fault lies in his concealment of the truth about himself. He is always misleading others, misinforming them about the person he knows himself to be. This is how

65

people become sick, as psychotherapists know. Much of the treatment in psychotherapy is concerned with getting a patient to open up and divest himself of painful, long-kept secrets. The cure comes when the patient stops misrepresenting himself and is able to talk honestly about himself to the people with whom he lives. The accurate portrayal of the self is of the utmost importance in establishing meaningful relationships and is, as I have said, an identifying criterion of a healthy personality.

People are aggressive and break the law for many different reasons. It is useless just giving them labels and locking them up. To help them one must know the real reason why they behave as they do, which they might not know themselves until they start talking honestly about themselves, taking away the screens they've put around their past. This is what I mean by seeking emotional knowledge about the person to be helped.

As I have said, emotional knowledge never comes from textbooks; it comes from living and feeling and observing yourself, not looking away from yourself as many people do, for instance, when they pretend that they do not feel jealous or angry or humiliated. It means facing up to yourself—to the kind of person you are—not making excuses. Accepting yourself is the first step to solving your problems. Also sharing your feelings with others can be very helpful. Self-disclosure will help others to solve their problems by encouraging them to be truthful about themselves too; this kind of honesty is catching as the young people at Lancaster House discovered.

Let me give you an example of what I mean by emotional knowledge from my own experience—something that actually happened to me recently while I was thinking about this problem. You may think it trivial—but it illustrates the way we can learn about our feelings.

Rosy, our large and lovable French herding dog, grabbed some sausages from the kitchen table while I was preparing lunch. I was furious with her. I had been looking forward to a "sausage and mash" lunch. I chased her, without the slightest hope of catching her—she's so swift on her feet—as she ran into the garden with the string of sausages trailing from her jaws. Then suddenly a picture came into my mind—a childhood memory that must have remained buried in the subconscious for I don't know how many years—forty-five at least! In my memory I saw an illustration in a magazine I read as a child of a fat apoplectic butcher, brandishing a stick—or was it a chopper?—as he chased a dog that had stolen some sausages from his shop. Suddenly I saw myself as ludicrous; and anger turned to laughter. If I hadn't been taught to laugh as a child, I wouldn't have been able to laugh at myself now.

Some people don't have happy memories. As children they were not allowed to experience delight. All their memories are of being hurt—of being told they were no good. Like the thin man in the fat man struggling to get out, there's love in people who are full of hatred, but they feel embarrassed or ashamed about their feelings. That's a terrible thing to happen to anybody, to grow up without feeling love or without being able to express it.

People who have been hurt in childhood are protesting all the time. All their words are angry words—they don't seem to see things straight and usually they have no sense of humour which, as most of us know, is the best kind of safety valve. They are, of course, protesting more about what happened to them in the past than about what is happening to them today. That is why their protests seem so unreasonable to us: they are not looking at things as they are today. If you create a void by denying love, it is inevitably going to be filled with hatred. Over the years their feelings of hatred have been reinforced because hatred has always been answered with hatred. That's all they know. So, of course, they are angry and, of course, they are sometimes violent. How else would you expect them to behave?

In a sense, every so-called anti-social act, political or otherwise, is protest. But "protest" is only the way we describe certain behaviour, and protest may not be the intention of the person himself. It may be more accurate to say that what he is doing is to try to transform an unbearable world into one that is bearable. The discontented seek to change the world ... by magic.

Let me quote the case of sixteen-year-old Julie who was expelled from school for stealing.

"I had to go to a psychologist quite often," she said, "but he couldn't work out why I stole, so he put me on to Dr. R. who sent me here." (Bracken House, a Richmond Fellowship hostel in Southampton.)

"Were you angry about something when you stole?"

"No, I don't know why I stole."

"Did you steal when you were very young?"

"I think I must have done. When you're little it's more or less natural to steal."

"Do you think it's because you were unhappy?"

"The last two times I was annoyed about something. Whether that's got anything to do with it ... The first time I was annoyed with Mum and Dad. I've forgotten what it was about so it couldn't have been very important. Mum was always nagging. I just can't stand people nagging me all the time. The second time was at school when I gave in two dinner tickets by mistake and I had to go and see the headmistress. She made me search through the week's dinner tickets to find out the day I'd given in two, so that I'd give in the other one on the right day. It was very stupid."

"Were the teachers very strict?"

"They were at the first school I went to after I'd passed the 11-plus. There were millions of rules. You just had to keep every one of them. School skirts weren't allowed to be six inches above the knee—*when* kneeling. You weren't allowed to speak in the main corridor which was the teacher's corridor. That school was very strict. Well, it was a grammar school, you see.

"Then I went to a secondary school ... and it was there one evening after my piano lesson that I saw the light shining on a tin in another girl's satchel. That attracted my attention and I whipped the tin out ... stuck it in my brief case. I didn't know what was in the tin."

Julie was trying to change a harsh world that denied her her freedom into one that presented her with gifts. The "magic" was stealing. In her present situation where she has more freedom and can discuss her problems with others, she will no longer feel the need to steal . . . to change the world by magic.

The young people at the Richmond Fellowship hostels all have one thing in common—they do not mind talking about themselves in an honest way; they feel secure enough now to allow themselves to be vulnerable; they have no secrets. In this way they are coming to terms with life—and feeling better for it in general health. As I have said, a person who is not afraid to say what he or she thinks is a healthy person. Concealment, holding back feelings, saying what is expected of you and not what you honestly think, and hiding the truth about yourself— all these things cause sickness.

This does not only apply to disturbed adolescents, but also to people, whoever they are, who smother themselves in their roles. They are not fully alive. They go on behaving in sickening ways and wonder why they are sick and unhappy; and they become aggressive when others expose any areas of weakness or vulnerability. To cure the sickness one must be able to talk honestly to someone, especially to members of one's own family. Allowing oneself to be vulnerable is not weakness; it requires a great deal of courage to reveal one's true self to others.

The young people in the Richmond Fellowship hostels are there because they have never previously been allowed to be themselves.

Man, I believe, has three basic needs, apart from his physical needs, that, if not satisfied, will lead to aggressive behaviour:

1. The need to believe in himself as unique; the need to be responsible for *himself*.
2. The need to feel an integrative part of the social and natural environment, with responsibilities to *others* and to the whole of nature.
3. The need to feel a purpose *beyond* himself and beyond his

social obligations: the need to feel that there is a higher authority than society.

I remember in my own case how miserable I was when, as a youngster of twenty I left home and tried to fend for myself in London. I remember writing to a friend—"I have plunged into the great vortex of life." But London wasn't so exciting as I had anticipated, which was mainly my fault. I became agonisingly self-conscious. In the tube I felt all eyes were upon me, and it was absolute hell to have to enter a room full of strangers. I did not talk to anyone out of choice, and I tried not to be noticed.

My trouble was that I felt I had to stand high in my *own* opinion or stand nowhere at all. It was not just conceit—it was a feeling of vulnerability. I was turning my back on life, because I felt I had something precious in me that would be destroyed if I allowed myself to live in the world of others. I was protesting all the time. Writing then was, for me, a form of protest. Reading was protest. Going to London was protest.

Many other young people are like the sort of person I was then not realising that, paradoxical though it may seem, it is possible to establish bonds through argument and conflict. It is better to take risks to establish a relationship than to isolate yourself from others. Self-isolation is very painful.

Not trusting yourself, you copy others; but you can never move into another's world completely. It is better to live honestly with someone than to try slavishly to be like that other person, even though he may seem to be a much better person than you are. Each of us has his or her own background of unique experience and can never be a carbon copy of someone else. A young person wants the world to be different. Of course he does —this is expected of youth. He feels he has something to contribute but he is undervalued. Although older people keep talking about the importance of communication, they refuse to listen to him. He looks around him and sees so many things that are wrong and unjust—so much selfishness. His feelings are right— people are often selfish and the world *is* in a mess—but he is taught to distrust his feelings. As a French writer said, *"Les choses sont contre nous"* (things are against us); facts are regarded as more important than feelings. And so distrusting his own feelings, a young man will start imitating others who seem to him to be strong and successful. He wants things to work out for him too. Part of his plan for a better world is his own personal goal of obtaining respect. Then he meets a girl. Then he marries. Then children arrive—and he worries about them and the mortgage. His dreams fade. He now has to face reality though he has his private thoughts, which he dare not talk about because his actions have separated him from his thoughts. But he grows up when he accepts responsibility for what he does. Then he can really be himself and do some good in the world; but unfortunately he does what almost everyone else does—he settles down and his own children grow up in the same way as he did, a stranger to himself.

10

Becoming a Real Person

THERE is also the important *physical* side of our behaviour to be taken into account. Adolescents are acutely conscious of physical differences between themselves and their friends. They worry about their shape and height, whether they have broad or narrow shoulders, their muscular development and so on.

Not all adolescents experience their period of rapid growth

at the same times. Some boys may grow suddenly at about the age of twelve and may become very lonely waiting for their friends to "catch up." Others may not experience this acceleration of growth until nearly seventeen. They may suffer feeings of inferiority and by way of compensation become very aggressive while they remain small compared with their friends.

Parents may find it difficult not to go on treating their adolescent sons and daughters as children even though the evidence of their own eyes shows that they are becoming adults. From a very early age every individual is bi-sexual, secreting both male and female hormones. At puberty the secretion of female sex hormones increases markedly in the case of most girls and there is a similar marked increase in male sex hormones in most boys. The increases in sex hormones has the effect of slowing the rate of physical growth; and consequently if sexual development is delayed, the limbs will grow to a disproportionate extent. Parents might regard the tall boy as an adult, whereas it is the small boy who may be sexually more mature.

The growth of facial hair on boys, and the onset of the menstrual period and development of breasts in girls, have great social significance but they are not very reliable indicators of adult physical development.

Sexual and physical development occurring at different times produce marked differences in physical stamina; some boys and girls experience unusual fatigue whilst others of the same age may be very energetic. It can have a damaging effect on personality development to accuse the boy or girl who is always tired, and who may stay in bed late, of laziness when in fact he or she is passing through a very difficult phase that calls for much sympathetic understanding.

Young adolescents who are sensitive about their appearance should be handled wisely and carefully; they need all your sympathy. So often some apparent physical defect or clumsiness due to a lack of co-ordination when a child grows up rapidly, may lead to aggressiveness in the adolescent and irritation in the parent. Knowing what is normal will help to prevent a lot of friction.

Many of the pop songs that appeal to young people are an expression of teenage feelings, such as the feeling of being isolated or helpless in a hostile world, or the young person's often-felt sense of impotency, or the feeling of ordinariness about the life around them which the great German writer Goethe described as "the deadly commonplace that fetters us all."

Consider this song by the Beatles, called *Real Nowhere Man* (written in 1965) about a character with whom many teenagers can identify—someone who is uncertain about who he is and where he is going. The song defines the problem in a way that appeals to the young and offers a solution :

> He's a real Nowhere Man,
> Sitting in his nowhere land,
> Making all his nowhere plans for nobody.
> Doesn't have a point of view,
> Knows not where he's going to,
> Isn't he a bit like you and me?
> Nowhere man please listen,
> You don't know what you're missing
> > Nowhere Man.
>
> The world is at your command.
> He's as blind as he can be,
> Just sees what he wants to see,
> Nowhere Man can you see me at all?
> Nowhere Man don't worry,
> Take your time, don't hurry,
> Leave it all till somebody else lends you a hand.

The Beatles' music shows a keen perception of the many emotional problems that confront the adolescent. Their lines have been described by Dr. T. Leland, an American psychiatrist, as "an existential interpretation or reality." A group of students in health education at Arizona State University found that the Beatles' songs were a valuable tool for involving students in the learning process, related to the subject matter of mental health. They described the songs and the principal emotional issues involved in the lyrics as follows :

1. *A Little Help From My Friends*
   The lyrics of this melody with the universal human need for acceptance and understanding. The educator will find this useful in setting the stage for a class discussion of the meaning of love.

2. *Try to See it My Way*
   This lyric concerns itself with communication empathy. The concept that tranquillity may be established if communication becomes possible is developed in these lyrics.

3. *I'm Only Sleeping*
   Here the Beatles present a testimonial for daydreaming. In these lyrics, the Beatles are closely aligned to the position of Dr. Paul Walters, Psychiatrist, Harvard University Health Center, who states : "Among late adolescents, disinterest is either a reaction to realistic impending defeat or a symptom of psychological difficulty centring around real confusion over the difference between competitiveness and injury, aggressiveness and aggression. It is not laziness, worthlessness or weakness." This lyric may serve to introduce an "avoidance of choice" as a personality trait.

4. *Real Nowhere Man*
   The lack of self identity is the psychological issue discussed in these lyrics. The educator might utilise this melody to deal with the issues in personality development facing the individual in the period of time between childhood and adulthood (adolescence).

5. *Yesterday*
Provides an excellent opportunity to discuss escapism, as the song lyrics suggest to the adolescent that regression to childhood would remove them from the agony of adolescence.

6. *Act Naturally*
Fantasy—This lyric suggests to the adolescent that success is possible without effort. The educator has the opportunity to utilise this song as an introduction to a group discussion of fantasy. That fantasy develops creativity but success needs training.

7. *She's Leaving Home*
This is an all-time Beatle hit which extols to the youthful listener that parents in the final analysis aren't really interested in the welfare of the child, but only about the image of their capability as a parent. This lyric may be used as a lead in to a discussion analysis of the importance of communication between generations, and the parental role in personality development.

8. *While My Guitar Gently Weeps*
This hauntingly beautiful melody concerns itself with the phenomenon of futility. The lyric is perhaps the heaviest of all Beatle dialogue since it reflects on the growing concern of the youthful generation that things (the organisation of society) are out of their control. The educator may utilise this lyric to discuss the impact of social conflict on personal mental health problems.

The adolescent has had no adult past. His past is his childhood, living at home, being entirely dependent on parents—and he wants to break away from them but does not know how. His parents and teachers will go on saying things to him "in his head," if not in fact, and one could describe childhood as a chronic condition that remains with us all our lives.

Character is formed at a time when one is completely vulnerable. An infant is at the mercy of two people who may know very little about the normal processes of development and may interfere with those processes. The brain undergoes the greater part of its growth after birth when it is exposed to the vicissitudes of the environment. Such a delicate instrument needs expert and careful attention and yet there are parents who are more careful with their car or washing machine than they are with a child's mind. The surprising thing is that so many children grow up without being unduly disturbed.

The so-called mature adult is usually known, not for the person he truly is, but for what he has done in the past, and for his position in life—he is the man who lives in a certain kind of house, owns a certain kind of car, married a schoolteacher or the doctor's daughter, plays golf or cricket, is keen on politics and so on. We build up a picture of him through knowing about his past, his job, his interests, his various relationships and his possessions. Rob him of all these things and there is not much left. Perhaps the person himself has not really grown up and is no wiser about his real identity that his teenage son or daughter.

Colin Wilson once described modern man as someone who looks in the mirror to adjust his tie—and sees nothing. He talks of a "black bag" covering the consciousness, preventing us from "glimpsing life as a torrent instead of a narrow, meandering, muddy stream ... The hawk is the most dangerous bird, yet when you put a black bag over its head it becomes completely docile. Human beings have a black bag over their consciousness." It is often said that a man is what he does, which is not really true—that is how the world sees him. I believe it is truer to say—though this doesn't apply to everyone—that a man is what he hides ... under the black bag.

When you talk to your wife or husband who is it you see? A real person or just your *idea* of your wife or your husband—your "better half" you might say, but still only a half. There is in such a relationship, as the psychiatrist R. D. Laing puts it, "a double absence." Even in the intimacy of marriage each partner may be concealing his or her true self from the other, and this is a cause of marital tensions and also a cause of confusion in children.

A man is what he hides. The world sees him playing games, conforming, obeying the law. Inside he's different. Only *he* knows it. How can he change the outside so that it reflects more truly what he feels inside? This is a question which few adults ask because to change means taking risks—it may mean changing a style of life that has become comfortable because it causes the least pain to yourself and others—or because you learn as you grow older that however much you try to change the outside you know that you cannot fight society alone; your personality (a word derived from the Greek *persona* meaning mask) is moulded by the circumstances in which you live and by the way others see you, and in the end you believe that you are in fact the sort of person others say you are. This doesn't necessarily have to happen; but I'm afraid it usually does. It requires a great deal of courage to be yourself.

The important point is that for the teenager there is at least the *possibility* of becoming a real person. But it's difficult, and the best advice we can give is :

1. Do small things well before trying to tackle big things. Don't try to get anywhere too soon.
2. Try to see people as they really are, not as you imagine them to be. Often when you are talking to someone you will find, if you think about it, that you are merely talking to your "idea" of that person, particularly if it's someone in authority; and admittedly you will sometimes find that you will get no help from the other person because he is smothered in his role. But if you can see this you won't be unhappy; you will try to see the face behind the mask.
3. Also try to see your situation—at home, school or work—as it really is. One hears a lot about "awareness" these days as if it's some kind of magical thing that just happens to you without effort. You are simply "turned on." And

that's why some are tempted to take drugs—because they imagine, as they often say, that pot or L.S.D., for instance, will give them "instant awareness." But it's a delusion to suppose this can happen. What drug-taking does is to cut you off from others.

Awareness means being aware of your total situation, which, of course, includes others. It means understanding your family and the people at work or school and understanding the way you interact with others to create a particular style of living or of working together.

The important thing is to try to improve relationships and that is by far the best way you can help yourself. In fact the only way to understand yourself is by trying to understand others—and that means all the people you are involved with in your life and all those who have influenced you in the past who were mainly responsible for the way you think and behave today. The moment you are born the world starts working on you and this goes on to the end. There is very little you can call your own.

4. Don't dismiss people by giving them labels. Try to understand them.

5. Trying to improve yourself as if no-one else existed will get you nowhere. Self-understanding is not turning the mind inwards; it's looking outside yourself at the world around you and at your own past—and, yes, at history too : at the way, for instance, your country's institutions have evolved because they exercise an important influence on your life; it's no use kicking against them if you don't understand them.

You may still be trapped in your own personal past, without realising it, just as countries are sometimes trapped in their history, so that you can't see very clearly what is happening to you in the present. So long as you stay in a trap you will go on fighting others and yourself.

The problems of living are mostly tied up with interpersonal relationships. They can often be traced back to faulty early conditioning. The way you relate to others in adult life is dependent to a large extent upon the emotional environment in which the first years of your life were passed when you came mainly under the influence of your parents. But you must not go on blaming parents for whatever may have gone wrong with your life; they too were largely the products of their environment. Instead of blaming them you should try to correct their mistakes. To prevent a repetition of old patterns of thought and behaviour it is essential to understand your own social and cultural background, which may have cast you in a superior or inferior role, and also the historical processes that created circumstances in which many were (and, I'm afraid, still are) neglected, rejected or exploited by society. You must also understand the way in which people of high character and genius—the great reformers, philosophers, artists and religious leaders—have overcome their circumstances and fought for the freedom which you now enjoy, or who have given us works of great beauty—poetry, architecture, music —that lift us above the pettiness and ugliness of life. There are a number of paths you can follow in life that will bring you rich rewards in love and friendship and they have already been signposted by the great men of the past . . .

> Lives of great men all remind us
> We can make our lives sublime,
> And departing leave behind us
> Footprints in the sands of time.

6. Try to see things for yourself. What is true must be *true* for you personally. Don't just agree because you think somebody may know more than you do. Work things out for yourself. Don't just follow others blindly—all the gurus, politicians, pop idols who say clever things. Listen by all means, but critically. Don't follow merely because it's the fashion or you like somebody's face or because of the

79

excitement somebody generates or because he offers you some dubious short cut to happiness.

7. When you talk of escape consider carefully what you are escaping from and where you are escaping to.

8. Find a girl or boy you can love but not possess, someone who can love you, too, simply for the person you *are* without wanting to possess you. Loving someone is establishing an I-Thou relationship in which the other's past is fully known and understood and does not go on bothering you. You can then both concentrate on living in the here and now. The present can only speak to you if the past is silent.

9. Be truly yourself—thoughtful, critical, honest to yourself and others, courteous, understanding, and remove all those chips from your shoulder and the barrier you may have put around yourself to protect your self-image. It's all a very painful process, I know. It requires, as I have said, courage to be yourself—but in the end you will find the effort has been worthwhile. Your most important task in life is to discover yourself.

10. Remember this : there can be no happiness without some anguish. There is happiness in struggle, even in pain and stress. A life of ease doesn't bring happiness. This is demonstrated by the fact that in London, for instance, there are more suicides in wealthy boroughs such as Hampstead and Westminster than in the poorer parts of the East End. Also, in spite of the anxiety felt during the war there were fewer suicides then than in peacetime. People talk about their right to be happy; but happiness has to be earned, sometimes through suffering. A person should be grateful for his difficulties. At the happiest time of one's life, in youth, one has more difficulties than at any other time.

The Excitement Game

IN America a movement has been started called Grey Lib—
meaning liberation for the older generation, because, the founder
believes, it is the older people who suffer most in our present
day society. To back up this campaign statistics are quoted
showing that the highest rate of recorded suicides is between
fifty-five and sixty-five, and that, according to some investiga-
tions, maximum prevalence of neurotic illnesses occur at the same
age.

The young talk of the "padlocked world" of their generation.
It is, however, probably more true to say that each generation
lives in its own padlocked world. Each generation shuts itself in
and puts up "keep out" notices. Instead of asking "*who* is to
blame?" we should be asking "*what* is to blame?" "Who?",
according to the young, is easy to answer. "It's the old of course!
They do not want to listen to the young, they have lost their
idealism and have become disillusioned and cynical. Older
people cannot adapt to new ways of thinking, cannot assimilate
new ideas. The older generation is too busy making money ..."
and so on.

What is to blame? That is also easy to answer—in a superficial
way. "The affluent society, of course! The greediness of everyone; the young are spoilt through having too much money; the
old don't take enough exercise and wear themselves out in 'the
rat race', ..." and so on.

For their part, the older generation are also asking questions—
questions like "Why all this emphasis on youth in the press and
on television? Why shouldn't as much attention be given to the
middle-aged?"

Everyone knows the answer, or part of the answer. Because, of course, the problems of youth are much more interesting and dramatic. Many suburban homes would be very dull places without the problems of youth to give them a little excitement. "Emotions are tightly constrained in the suburban home," writes Dr. Cyril Smith, Director of Studies of the Department of Youth Work at Manchester University... "youth offers a contrast... that appears exciting, unrestrained, engaged in conflicts with authority, and deeply involved in meaningful relationships with the opposite sex."

Full-employment in the post-war years put more money into the pockets of the young. A new market was created for those who had something to sell to the young, who were then cultivated by the mass media, fashion designers, gramophone record companies, entertainers and others. Bob Dylan might sing about "The times they are a-changing," but changing times made a lot of money both for him and for Columbia Records. But who cared? Everyone was happy. A swinging world was better than a violent, impoverished one.

It was thought that with the abolition of much of the poverty in the country violence would disappear. But we were wrong. Our optimism was based on studies in the thirties and forties which showed that there was a concentration of crime and delinquency in slum areas where there was a great deal of poverty, bad housing and unemployment. But since then, in spite of the expansion of social services and the reduction in the number of impoverished families, the figures for crime and delinquency have risen to new peaks.

It was only after the last war that society really became aware of a new kind of problem. The old were tired. They preached the virtues of the steady job, the insurance policy and a secure family life. But there did not seem to be any causes left for young people to fight for; young people felt that nothing was happening or likely to happen. The answer to this situation was for young people to invent the Excitement Game.

John Osborne in *Look Back In Anger* was the first to draw

attention to the problem . . . "Let's pretend we're human beings, and that we're actually alive, just for a while; What do you say? Let's pretend we're human. Oh, brother, it's such a long time since I was with anyone who got enthusiastic about anything . . . I suppose people of our generation aren't able to die for good causes any more. We had all that done for us, in the thirties and forties, when we were still kids. There aren't any good brave causes left. If the big bang does come, and we all get killed off, it won't be in aid of the old-fashioned grand design. It'll be for the Brave New-nothing-very-much-thank you. About as pointless and inglorious as stepping in front of a bus."

The first casualty in the Excitement Game was described by the Underground writer and poet Jeff Nuttall: "In 1953 a boy was stabbed to death on Clapham Common. He was no slum boy, nor was his killer. He came from a seemingly happy family in a seemingly comfortable home. The murder was not done for gain or revenge or the hand of a girl. . . . The Excitement Game was unrelated to 'constructive' living. Theft was understandable. Revenge was understandable, but the principle of excitement was not. . . ."

Increasing numbers of young people started doing things "for kicks"—from tearing up plants in Municipal parks, stuffing chewing gum and lolly sticks in telephone coin-slots to "queer-bashing" on Wimbledon Common which resulted, in one notorious case, in a young homosexual being beaten to death.

In America the situation was—and still is—much worse. The way the Excitement Game can lead eventually to the most appalling crimes is illustrated by the story of the brutal Sharon Tate killings. It all began with a group of young people, mostly girls (Charles Manson's "Family") who, in their search for excitement, established a commune in the Californian desert with the aim of "creating a new form of tribal music and spiritually." But this aim was soon forgotten and the commune turned to dope-peddling and extortion. Inspired by the Beatles' film, "The Magical Mystery Tour," they travelled around in a bus, which they painted black.

Charles Manson, the leader, was raised in the U.S. prison system. He was a sinister, insecure character whose personal magnetism attracted other weak young people around him. He promised his followers liberation, but they became his slaves. "I'm a very positive force," he told a lawyer after his arrest. "I'm a very positive field. I collect negatives."

In their search for thrills the girls learnt from Manson how they could expand their consciousness by what he called "getting the fear." It was, he said, an exquisite physical experience. "I pick a rich house. I don't steal, I walk into the house and the fear hits you like waves. It's almost like walking on waves of fear."

He also advised his girls to do the unexpected. "No sense makes sense. You won't get caught if you've got no thought in your head."

Soon the girls started "crawling" (the word they used) into houses and stealing jewellery and fur coats, not because they particularly wanted them, but just for the thrill of committing a crime. They sought bigger and bigger thrills but nothing satisfied —until in the end they murdered "to get the fear."

A lot of mugging is carried out for the same reason. At the centre of a mugging gang there is often an unstable boy, like Manson, with a highly troubled background—a violent or alcoholic father is common—and he usually has his lieutenants, boys whose backgrounds are usually unhappy rather than violent.

The leader and his lieutenants form the nucleus of the gang but the trouble is that, like Manson, they usually attract weak characters around them, boys from backgrounds that are not generally regarded as disturbed or abnormal. They are boys— and, sadly, girls too these days—who are looking for excitement. It is a tragedy that these impressionable youngsters—the outer rings of the gangs—may go the same way as the tougher gang leaders, ending up in prison or borstal.

A boy explaining how mugging starts said, "Well, it starts at school. You and your mates pounce on a timid boy and rob him of his dinner money. It's just a giggle . . ."

It is not so much poverty as boredom that leads to this kind of crime. And this is the view of Chief Superintendent Jim Collie, head of the Young Offenders section of Scotland Yard, who said that 70 per cent of juvenile crime was committed by groups of three or more, but their case papers showed that most of their offences occurred spontaneously, without any predetermined plan, supporting the view that idleness, boredom and crime are directly linked.

Thus the earlier theories about poverty and crime seem irrelevant today. What had been left out of the reckoning was the part played by the imagination of young people. We can see the Excitement Game as a new way of defining certain aspects of teenage violence. It is a new theory which gives meaning to behaviour that many would regard as "cruel and pointless," and adds a new dimension to the problem of violence. And the theory itself—doing violent things for kicks or "looking for aggro"—is translated into reality by others when they hear about it, which sociologists call the "amplification" of a problem.

There are those who believe that the young today have been moulded by what people of an older generation absorbed of the teachings of Freud and his followers. So much so, in fact, that it sometimes seems many youngsters have deliberately imitated text-book models, transposing psychological theories into conduct. There are, for instance, youngsters who seem to be quite proud of the fact that they are paranoic or sadistic or suffering from "identity confusion"; there is a dramatic outer display of what at one time used to be considered as inner secrets.

Just how strong is this outer display of "disturbance" characteristics is well illustrated by the experience my wife (herself a teacher) had when she went to talk about aggression with some young people at CURE (National Addiction and Research Institute). My wife went as observer, taking a tape recorder with her, and she was taken straight into the middle of a group session.

The room where the meeting was being held was bare; it overlooked King's Road, Chelsea. Sitting and standing around was a collection of what she describes as "hippies, young East End toughs, Chelsea types and two older men who, as I discovered later, joined the sessions to try to draw people out. Nobody offered me a chair. What followed was unbelievable. Without feeling any aggression towards anyone, my very presence created a riot of mocking behaviour. Anyone else, I'm sure, would have walked out immediately, but this was the kind of aggressive behaviour I had come to talk about. It took some time before it was quiet enough to start a discussion and switch on the tape."

My wife tried to avoid imposing her views on the group and thought she could stand on one side while the others did all the talking, but this objective approach proved quite impossible as the following extracts from the transcript show :

Alan (describing what happens at group sessions) : Violence is absolutely taboo. I mean physical violence . . . we translate it into a kind of verbal thing. What we are trying to do in general is to establish better lines of communication between people.

John : They call us the Chelsea gang and we go marching up and down King's Road being violent towards people, but we don't actually hit them. We just sort of do violent things to make them think about themselves.

Observer : Like what?

John : Well, we're just having fun influencing people.

Observer : In what way?

John : Well, we're showing a lot of people that we're having fun.

Observer : Why do you often behave in an aggressive way towards the older generation?

John : There ain't been no wars for our generation. Not like the others—the First World War and . . .

Observer : What about Vietnam and Northern Ireland?

Alan : Yeah, but look—why would we want to go over and kill a lot of Paddies? Or go and kill a load of chinks up in Vietnam. It's not our war. That's America's war . . ,

Observer: You'd like your own war, would you?

Alan: Yeah.

Observer: But you said you were trying to translate violence into a verbal thing.

Alan: Oh yeah, but that's only sort of like the Hippies, isn't it?

John: You get a gang of Skinheads walking down the road and they see a couple of Greasers. They're not going to say, "You lousy bums!' They're going to go and do something about it. Well, if they've got any sense they would. . . . The marvellous thing about this place is that me and Alan can communicate . . .

Peter (to the observer): I don't understand why you're here. There was a lot of aggressive behaviour directed at you when you came in.

Observer: Well, I'm here to find something out . . . How you feel towards me is of no importance whatever.

Bill: Yeah, I think that's the trouble. I wasn't feeling aggressive towards you. It's just the idea of someone coming in here with a tape recorder and setting themselves up as an observer . . . I'd have understood if there'd been an actual reaction. I think maybe that was a good way of presenting your aggression towards us . . . in fact, I think you've asked for it.

Observer: If I'd known what I was coming into . . .

Bill: No if's. No if's. I think 'if's' are very extraordinary.

Alan: Actually, it's very funny, because it's never happened before. We've never shown aggression to anyone who comes. Very, very rarely. We're always incredibly polite and rather than show aggression we cut off. Showing aggression verbally is better than cutting off, because when you cut off you pretend that the other person doesn't exist. Nothing could be more negative than cutting off.

Observer: What are you upset about?

Bill: I'm quite upset at the way you set things up for yourself. Then I'm quite upset that I didn't cotton on much quicker to what you wanted . . . you accept that we haven't been fair to you and that's an end to it.

From this incident with the tape recorder we see that in trying to understand human behaviour it is impossible to be objective. The situation that was being observed was a situation in which the observer was also involved and the fact that the tape recorder was there also had an influence on people's behaviour. We saw the same kind of thing happening in Bangladesh when the presence of television cameras influenced events. The observer and his equipment become part of the "scene."

What my wife learnt from this encounter was something about her own reactions. It was subjective or emotional knowledge; but it was knowledge that could only be gained with the help of others who presented themselves as subjects, not as objects being interrogated. The youngsters at first were upset because they felt my wife was not reacting sympathetically, but they did not help very much because they saw her as an object in her role as interrogator. She was to them the authoritarian stereotype (with her uniform of blouse and costume), a scapegoat who helped to strengthen the bonds of the others.

In fairness to CURE (in case I should have given the impression that they are a gang of unruly adolescents), I must say that on the whole they seem to be doing an extremely good job. A lot of creative work goes on there and very disturbed young people are being helped to overcome their difficulties by attending regular discussion sessions in which everyone is encouraged to speak freely. And part of the therapy seems to be that no one has to be polite or say what he does not honestly feel. As we saw with the Richmond Fellowship, when you are dealing with disturbed adolescents you cannot have too many rules.

12

Adventure Playgrounds

"The child faced with a difficult choice between
his own delight experience and the experience of
approval from others, must generally choose
approval from others, and then handle his delight
by repression or letting it die, or not noticing it or
controlling it by will-power. In general, along with
this will develop a disapproval of the delight
experience, or shame and embarrassment and
secretiveness about it, with finally the inability to
experience it . . ."

Abraham Maslow

A child in his anxiety to adjust to adult standards of behaviour
is afraid to be himself—which means he is afraid of his finest
impulses. Adults see only the hell in the unconscious, but for the
child there is only heaven. Adults see children as men and
women and are intent on training them, as they say, to be useful
citizens. They are thus robbing them of their present and also of
the talent they have to enjoy life—"the mere living."

The picture we have of childhood is coloured by what happens
afterwards. We see what is going to happen, not what is happening now, we worry about the child's future and we go on
worrying until he is an adolescent and he leaves home. It is
always the future we are concerned about.

A child, however, sees what he sees—nothing more. Everything is fun, except when he hears the word "don't," and in
having fun he begins to understand himself and the world
around him; he understands through his own direct experience.

Gradually this ability to live in the present fades as he grows older and in adolescence he becomes confused : he is torn between what he *wants* to do and what he *ought* to do.

Let me go back to childhood again with another memory. I was standing three feet tall in my sailor suit—on that same pavement in Birkenhead where I rolled balls of tar—and watched a swirling mass of clouds in the afternoon sky. It was just before tea; so in the memory there is also the smell of hot buttered toast. (If anybody gave me an association test now and threw the word "clouds" at me, I would instantly respond with "hot buttered toast"). I was not alone as I gazed entranced at those clouds. There was a friend called Norman standing beside me, sharing my pleasure. That was a peak experience— the delight experience that every child knows—when we discovered those clouds together. It was a moment that would never come again, though we didn't think in those terms; we didn't live in passing time.

And here is another memory that illustrates how the delight experience is repressed. It was a cold winter's day, frosty but kindly. I was sliding on an icy patch in the school playground when I fell and broke a leg. My father was furious with the school, accusing them of negligence. Why wasn't there anyone around to look after the children in the playground? Why couldn't someone keep an eye on them? He threatened to sue the school for damages . . . and from then onwards, alas, there was always a teacher in attendance in the playground. She was merely there to tell us what we couldn't do. We couldn't fight, we couldn't play marbles—that was gambling!—we couldn't swing on the gate, we couldn't play outside the headmaster's study . . . there were so many things we couldn't do and we were all bursting with energy after being cooped up in a classroom for so long, trying among other things to solve problems like : if it takes five minutes to fill a ten gallon tank with soda water, how long will it take to fill fifty pint bottles?

Well, that was a long time ago. Things are a little different now, I hope; but there are still many who fail to appreciate that children must have somewhere to go where they can truly be themselves, where they don't have to repress the delight experience for fear of disapproval, where they can feel the texture of things and use their eyes, where they can feel their life throbbing in every limb ... and where they can live without effort with "what is."

As I said in the last chapter there are many young people these days who just cannot find an outlet for their energies, having nowhere to go except on the streets for excitement and adventure. They have never learnt to play in a constructive or creative way mainly because in our big cities we neglect the needs for children's play space. The schools are closed and empty soon after four, so where can children go? We are going to spend £30m over the next two years on nursery education, but nothing at all is set aside for the most deprived sector of society today: i.e. the children of our inner-city areas who have virtually no play space at all.

Recently—at the time of going to press—I have been closely connected with Bishop Trevor Huddleston's "Fair Play for Children" campaign, handling the public relations. The aim of the campaign is to create a lobby for children at least as effective as that for cars.

"Children," said Trevor Huddleston at a press conference to launch the campaign, "are being killed in Britain every year while playing on the roads and in their homes because housing and road development have deprived them of play space."

The day before the conference I made arrangements for the B.B.C. to take a film at Spitalfields Adventure Playground, a most exciting place consisting of all kinds of weird and wonderful contraptions made by the children themselves. You don't see such things in the normal playground. The adventure playground keeps changing. The children knock things down and then build something new under the sympathetic eye of a play leader; nothing stays the same: all the time there are interesting and exciting things to do.

Unfortunately, on the day of the film it was raining (it was, in fact, one of the worst days of the year) and I was afraid there wouldn't be many children in the playground. And, in any case, most of the children would be at school at 2 p.m. when the B.B.C. wanted to take the film. I spoke to the playleader, Alan Kirk, about this, and he said, "The only children who will be here will be the truants." He added, "It's better for them to be here than on the streets ... But don't worry. I'll arrange something."

Alan got the co-operation of the headmaster of a local school, not 200 yards away, and at two o'clock precisely hundreds of children came swarming into the playground; and all their smiling faces made it seem like a sunny day. They weren't worried about the weather. They thought it was much more fun slopping around in an adventure playground than being stuck in a centrally-heated classroom.

The Bishop himself, although he had a streaming cold at the time, joined the throng in the rain and seemed to be enjoying himself as much as anyone. In such conditions good relationships between young and old are fostered, providing no one attempts to "organise" the fun.

I was amused to see one little Jamaican girl approach the Bishop and, taking hold of the gold cross that hung from his neck, say, "Cor! that must cost a lot of money." "Yes, indeed," said the Bishop. "It's very valuable, but it's not mine." One had the feeling that, if only he could, he would sell it to provide money for the playground. The playground was, in fact, going to close down in the New Year when, on the same day as the film was taken, the Bishop found someone to donate £2,000. "This is a wonderful day for us," said Alan Kirk. "I was going to try and borrow £50 to keep going."

The following day we had our press conference, but unfortunately it coincided with the publication of the Government White Paper on Education, so many of the journalists who had accepted invitations to the conference went instead to hear what Mrs. Thatcher had to say at a conference she had called only twenty-four hours before. We had been planning our conference for a fortnight. It seemed a bit unfair. Still, a B.B.C. camera team was there in St. Bride's, Fleet Street, where the conference was held, and they filmed an interview with the Bishop.

The sad part of this story is that at the end of the day, when hundreds of children and the young people who work in the adventure playground were looking forward to seeing themselves on the "box" and when all of us connected with the Bishop's campaign were hoping for some useful publicity, the B.B.C. decided to drop the story from their main news. I rang the news room afterwards, "I'm sorry about that," said a producer. "It's just one of those things that happen. There was Mrs. Thatcher, and then news came through at five-thirty about the verdicts of the Angry Brigade trial. There just wasn't time to show the film."

The Bishop had been saying at the press conference that all of us get our priorities wrong. In my view an example of this was the B.B.C. decision. Mrs. Thatcher's White Paper and the Angry Brigade verdicts were important, but there were other fairly trivial items of news that took up valuable time : children's play space was not, it seems, considered important. This sort of thing happens, not out of ill-will, but because people live by rules, in this case the rules that dictate what makes news.

But far, far worse than the B.B.C. decision, of course, is the way we put cars and garages before children in planning new housing estates. As an example of this, on an estate in Sheffield there are car parking spaces for 91 per cent of the houses, though only 47 per cent of the people on the estate own cars. The only provision for children's play is a small paved area and there are no other social amenities. (This, in fact, is stated in a Government publication : the Department of the Environment : "The Estate Outside the Dwelling".)

Can you wonder that vandalism is a big problem on that estate? And yet some people there blame—not the planners, but young people for the vandalism.* The planners themselves do

---

* Vandalism could be described as the way someone "makes his mark." Some schoolboys do this by carving their initials on their desks; lovers make their marks on trees. But where there are no trees a young person may make a mark which says "No" to the concrete jungle in which he has to live.

not deliberately set out to hurt children : they are also men who obey rules (they know, for instance, about the provision of garage space because it is in the rules), so the only answer to the problem of playspace is to make it a mandatory requirement.

It is rather sad that, generally speaking, people don't behave well unless the law compels them to or unless there's a rule of some sort taught in childhood. This is because, as I have been saying all along, we don't see what is happening in the world (we don't see unless we are told by those who do). Most of the time we are not fully aware of what we are doing because we live our lives mainly by rules, and this probably stems from the fact that in childhood we never develop what Sartre calls "reflective awareness"—i.e. awareness that is immediate and spontaneous, which can only be learnt in an unstructured environment such as an adventure playground. The planners make their plans without thinking. They may be sorry afterwards when it is too late to repair the damage. To be "reflectively" aware is to have your afterthoughts first.

Let me give you another figure. In Newcastle £20,000 a month is spent to secure schools against vandalism. Surely, law and order could be achieved at a different price, including better play provision.

"With land at £500,000 to £1,000,000 an acre in London and comparably high in other cities at present," says Ed Berman, Director of Inter-Action, "who will set it aside for the 'unproductive' (of rates, rents and appreciation) function of play? Moreover, spontaneous play is even messy, and in a neighbourhood of clean glass and concrete this is intolerable to some."

An answer to the Excitement Game invented by young people because their lives are so dull (including some children who are now risking their lives playing "chicken" across motorways) would be the creation of many more adventure playgrounds— community projects, consisting of indoor and outdoor facilities— in which all age groups can play a part. Young people should also be encouraged to join Outward Bound courses and adventure schools where they can take part in many different activities, including water skiing, mountain rescue work, mine shaft exploration, pony trekking and archery. There is not enough publicity about these adventure schools. They are a positive answer to the problem of violence.

13

Who is Normal?

LET us make a list of all the people who are blamed for the violence in society today. The exercise is revealing because it ends in a big question mark—it doesn't really contribute very much to the solution of the problem . . .

PARENTS : For not being strict enough, giving their children too much freedom; for their confusion, their failure to provide good models; or for not being affectionate enough, insisting that they know best, always laying down rules and never listening to what their children have to say.

SCHOOLTEACHERS : For the same reasons : allowing children to get the better of them, not being firm enough; for neglecting the shy or dull child and concentrating on the bright ones in the class. One doesn't hear so much criticism nowadays of teachers who are too strict or cruel—though neglect, of course, is a form of cruelty.

POLITICIANS : For not being concerned enough; for mouthing

platitudes and leaving it at that; for not giving a lead; for making promises they don't keep. They promise us heaven, but we know very well they are more likely to create hell. For playing party politics all the time, every one of them with his eye on a ministerial appointment.

THE POLICE : For not being tough enough; or for being too tough, particularly with youngsters; for spending too much time harassing motorists and not enough time fighting serious crime.

INDUSTRIALISTS AND BUSINESSMEN (Capitalists, Conservatives): For being acquisitive, materialistic—"getting a quid without going to quod;" for not caring what they are doing to the environment; for exploiting people.

THE WORKING CLASS (Communists, Socialists, Trade Unionists): For being greedy, not caring what they are doing to the economy, always demanding higher wages; for their hypocrisy— they'd like to be rich themselves. When they get into the House of Lords, as a few of them do, you'll find them knocking back whisky with the best of them!

RELIGIOUS LEADERS : For being more concerned about the Church than about people; for their failure to meet the spiritual needs of the younger generation; for their blindness, hypocrisy, aloofness.

JOURNALISTS : For not being serious enough; for the way they exaggerate and distort the news, putting all the emphasis on sex, money and violence.

YOUNG PEOPLE THEMSELVES : For their lack of respect for themselves and others; for being self-centred, unprincipled and obsessed with sex.

So everybody is to blame? Or is nobody to blame? Is there perhaps some sinister force at work in society—a kind of social cancer? Who we consider to blame depends mostly on who we are and where we live : our class, religion, occupation and age. We rarely blame ourselves. We push a problem out of our minds by blaming one particular segment of society, not usually our own.

We also make judgments according to what we regard as "normal" and "abnormal" behaviour—and this also depends to a large extent on who we are, where we live, when we live and how we live. If we had lived before the social reformer Wilberforce started campaigning against slavery, no doubt we would have regarded slavery as normal (as St. Paul did) and might even have looked up to people who could afford slaves just as some of us look up to people today who own Rolls Royces and Jaguars, status symbols of our age. Questioning the existence of God or the dogma of the Church was heresy at one time, punishable by torture or death. Probably Dr. Robinson, the former Bishop of Woolwich, would then have been burnt at the stake for some of the views expressed in his best-selling religious book, *Honest to God.*

Today there are those who are questioning our definitions of "normality" and "abnormality" and taking a closer look at the labels we attach to people. Are they *correct* descriptions? There are those who talk about the "myth" of mental illness—calling someone insane, they say, is a convenient way of dismissing a problem—and others who talk about crime as a sickness and sickness as a "role"—the sick role: i.e. escaping from unbearable tensions in a way that is acceptable to society, giving comfort to others who know that they too, when pressures build up, can escape into sickness, and also allowing the pressures to be kept up—very important in a highly competitive society.

The way we treat our sick, and also those whom we describe as deviant, influences the behaviour of those whom we regard as healthy and normal. There have been various sociological studies showing that deviant behaviour may be induced and sustained by a group and helps to maintain group equilibrium. The sociologist Jock Young points out that the sick role is common in drug taking because of the advantages to the individual himself and because of the pressures of outsiders who insist on viewing the drug taker in such light. The way a society responds to deviance—i.e. defines its deviants—can tell us something about that society. Or, to put it another way, an explanation of conformity leads to an explanation of deviance.

The psychiatrist R. D. Laing, whose views have had an important influence on the attitudes of many young people today, is one of those who do not see most of what we call mental illness as an illness at all, except in the sense that is the suffering of growth. He looks for "reasons" in behaviour that is generally described, and in a way dismissed, as "deviant," "neurotic," or "psychotic," and often finds that in the situation in which the sufferer finds himself his behaviour is in fact "reasonable"—for him it may be the only possible solution.

Thus a young man whose mother won't allow him to grow up may become aggressive towards her because in his situation it is the only means left to him of breaking away from her. Society has an idea of what the mother/son relationship should be—an ideal one; and the ideal is often regarded as "normal" which, of course, it isn't—so *any* son who attacks *any* mother is regarded as "abnormal." A newspaper headline might read, "Son Attacks Mother in Lonely Farmhouse." Our emotions are aroused. Immediately this conjures up for us the image of a kind, sweet mother (normal) being attacked by a vicious son (abnormal). That's the picture we have in our minds—and we are appalled. How could a son possibly attack his mother? The newspaper plays on our emotions, and following the journalist's dictum that you mustn't look too closely or "the story will crumble," may give only the mother's version of the incident, suitably embellished to tear at the heart strings.

Take the case of Mary, who in her teens was diagnosed as schizophrenic. Her parents, feeling helpless and instinctively ashamed, took her to an institution. In this way they pushed her out of their minds and never went back for her; and for about twenty years Mary lived in and out of one dreary mental hospital after another. On the occasions when she was released she found it impossible to adjust to life outside and usually went on some senseless shoplifting spree. Doctors held out no hope of a permanent cure.

Then, after stealing three coats, it was felt that Mary should be taught a lesson and sent to prison. And this is what would have happened to her if a probation officer had not pleaded her case and advised that she should be sent to a Richmond Fellowship hostel.

In the hostel Mary met young people like those I have already described at Lancaster House, who had suffered harrowing experiences similar to hers. Her past was forgotten—nobody wanted to know about it. For the first time she was treated as an adult and taught to be responsible for her actions. She was helped to "re-invent" herself. In this way she escaped the grey world of the insane and made her way back into society.

We think we know what is meant by "sick" and "insane" and are not impressed by theories that question what we regard as commonsense. I am reminded of the limerick—

> There was an old woman of Deal
> Who said that pain wasn't real—
> But if I sit on a pin
> And it punctures my skin,
> I dislike what I fancy I feel.

But, of course, it is not the reality of the illness that is being questioned but its cause which is implicit in the diagnosis. Sick, mad and bad have social connotations.

New ideas are not popular among the middle-aged. Young people are attracted to them because they are *new*; the opposite is the case with older people who view them with suspicion. This leads to conflict. Most of us have worked out some kind of *modus vivendi* by the time we are forty, or even before, and any disturbance to the way we live and think upsets us. That is the crux of the problem. We cling onto our beliefs because they are woven into the fabric of our lives from the very start and mean only what the clock on the mantelpiece or the slippers on the hearth mean to an old man—the comfort of familiar things. Ideas can be possessions just like our furniture or cars. In fact we sometimes talk of our ideas, beliefs and so on as the "furniture" of the mind.

Another problem is the problem of the man who is a doctor, a judge, a psychiatrist: the problem of how we see him and of how he sees himself which makes us interact with him in an almost predictable way. It is always *the* doctor, *the* judge, *the* psychiatrist—not a person at all. "I'm going to see the doctor," we say. It is the archetypal wise man we are thinking of—someone who doesn't really exist, someone we have invented. We don't, of course, see him as sick. But a good case could be made out that we are all sick in one way or another (war and violence in society are symptoms of our sickness), but we don't see the sickness because it is "socially patterned"—i.e. our culture provides patterns which allow us to live with our sickness. The psychiatrist Erich Fromm explained this concept of socially patterned sickness as follows: "Suppose that our Western culture movies, radios, television, sports events and newspapers ceased to function by only four weeks. With these main avenues of escape closed, what would be the consequences for people thrown back upon their own resources? I have no doubt that in this short time thousands of nervous breakdowns would occur, and many more thousands of people would be thrown into a state of acute anxiety, not different from the picture which is diagnosed clinically as 'neurosis'."

Among schizophrenics there are said to be many who started life as "good" children. There is something wrong with the docile, obedient child who never cries and is always anxious to please. There are two extremes: the child who is "too good to be true" and the child who, in an unhappy home, is always getting into trouble, is quarrelsome, disobedient, intractable— the sort of child of whom parents say, "We can't do anything with him."

It is, however, normal for a child to be naughty. His naughtiness is in fact often encouraged by parents, even when they tell him to "behave himself" because the admonition is accompanied by a half-smile of approval. What they are approving of is the child's natural, instinctive behaviour that often ignores adult rules. We all know about the "honesty" of a child who sometimes lets you down in company by innocently revealing family "secrets." He doesn't, of course, know the rule about loyalty to the family or about tact—sparing others' feelings —or many of the other rules of good behaviour: he has to be constantly reminded to wash his hands before eating, to say "thank you" and "please" and so on and so forth. There are hundreds of rules we take for granted, but the child doesn't.

Naughtiness means disobedience. . . . "I keep telling you not to do that. Why do you keep on doing it? If you do it again, I'll send you to bed." This is one of the ways we condition a child to do what we want him to. If there weren't any rules to disobey, children would never be naughty. It is interesting that a boy prodigy, who was educated at home by his Montessori-trained mother, didn't know the meaning of the word naughty—it just wasn't part of his vocabulary. The boy, who was being interviewed for a B.B.C. documentary, was admonished by a cameraman for splashing paint over the camera. "You're a naughty boy," chided the cameraman. "What's naughty?" asked the boy in wide-eyed innocence.

There are behaviour patterns that one expects at different stages of individual development. What is normal at one age may be abnormal at another. For instance, nail-biting is more normal than abnormal at the age of nine to twelve, but abnormal in an adolescent. Similarly bed-wetting or thumb-sucking, which is not uncommon in children and nothing really to get alarmed about, is abnormal in adolescence. The naughtiness of a child who stamps his feet when he can't get his own way would be described—correctly—as "infantile" in an adult; but it is normal for the adolescent—at least occasionally—to come into conflict with authority, particularly with parents, because this is one of his ways of asserting his independence and responsibility for himself. Adolescence itself has its different phases, though the boundaries are sometimes blurred. In early adolescence there is a search for identity and identification, and a boy may join a peer group in order to avoid conflict with his father; and at this time far greater value is placed on emotions than reason— feelings are seen to be spontaneous, free, honest, dramatic where- as reason is associated with harshness, rigidity, concealment and routine. In the middle stage of adolescence a firm feeling of identity develops (though there are some who have a protracted identity conflict which may go on for years) and a boy may seek an adult male companion or may identify with a mature woman. The way he sees people behaving towards one another, in his own circle at school, university or work, becomes a part of his own way of life.

Generally speaking, among young people of all ages there seem to be two main types. There are the majority who lean towards conformity and don't have a burning desire to change the world (though they may sometimes talk about it in clichés picked up from others) and there is the minority—often earnest, highly intelligent young people—who instead of taking over prescribed forms of behaviour seek to modify them. It is this minority who cause a great deal of the tension in society because society is reluctant to allow too much individual initiative. Throughout history there have always been the compliant and defiant. Every age throws up its defiant young idealists (it is believed by some that there is a constant ratio of one to twenty in this class*) and it is among the defiant that great leaders and reformers are to be found. A good example was Bernard Shaw who said, "All men are in a false position in society until they have realised

* Colin Wilson in *The Occult* (1971) discusses what he calls the dominant 5 per cent. He quotes Bernard Shaw who once asked the explorer, Henry Stanley, how many of his men could take over the leadership of his party if he, Stanley, were ill. "One in twenty," said Stanley. "Is that figure exact or approximate?" "Exact." Wilson points out that the dominant 5 per cent was rediscovered by the Chinese during the Korean War. Wishing to economise on man-power, they decided to divide their American prisoners into two groups, the enterprising ones and the passive ones. They soon discovered that the enterprising soldiers were exactly one in twenty. When this dominant 5 per cent were removed from the rest of the group, the others could be left with almost no guard at all.

their possibilities and imposed them on their neighbours." Instead of "all men are . . ." Bernard Shaw should have said, "Some men feel" (as he himself probably did in his youth) "that they are in a false position . . ."

The more we think about it the more difficult does it become to explain the difference between normal and abnormal; and before we start giving people labels we should try to get this straight in our minds. It is as well to remember that the meaning of the word *ab*-normal is *from* (Latin *ab*) the normal—i.e. the abnormal develops from normal behaviour. Or you could put it another way. The abnormal is the normal—*plus* something else, just as the sub-normal is minus something. The "plus" factor is some interference with normal development or you might say it is an obstruction that dams the river or diverts it over inhospitable terrain, preventing it from flowing gently to the sea.

The relationship between normal and abnormal behaviour is also explained in the following proposition : *"Mental forms which lie behind the delusions and odd behaviour of the mentally ill have an affinity with those which inform the thoughts and 'normal' behaviour of others in society."* In other words, the very things that make us normal somehow get twisted into the abnormal.

A Sunday afternoon exercise I once set my own family was to define "abnormal"—an exercise which I respectfully suggest other parents might usefully set their own teenage children instead of offering solutions themselves. The conclusions we came to were interesting. We decided that an abnormal person was someone 1. who because of his self-image of toughness or feelings of insecurity or inadequacy threatens, harms or takes the life or property of others; 2. who makes excessive demands on others; 3. who over-plays a part—e.g. over-conforms; 4. whose intelligence or creativity is misdirected into anti-social behaviour; 5. who cuts off, disengages or opts out of society—this does not include members of a monastic order or of some other idealistic self-contained group.

It seems to me that most people whom society regards as abnormal fall into one of these categories. Examples are :

1. *People who threaten, harm or take life or property:* Drunken drivers, pyromaniacs, child molesters, rapists, thieves, vandals, murderers.

2. *People who make excessive demands:* Alcoholics; drug addicts; nymphomaniacs (i.e. women who are always craving for sexual pleasures); people who threaten or feign suicide without serious intention—to attract attention to themselves; their attempts are half-hearted.

The poet Sylvia Platt was an example of someone who feigned suicide—not expecting to die, but taking the risk. When she accidentally succeeded she left a note giving the telephone number of her doctor. She wrote a poem once in which she said dying was an art . . . "I do it exceptionally well." I myself once found a young man who had made a half-hearted attempt at suicide on Hampstead Heath. He had slashed his wrists, but hadn't done a good job (there was a lot of blood but only superficial grazes); and although he had hidden himself behind some bushes his groans attracted my attention, as they were meant to.

Other examples of people who make demands (though through no fault of their own) are the chronic and incurably sick (physically abnormal). The physically abnormal often compensate for their abnormality by being aggressive; so when someone is aggressive or bad-tempered one should watch out for signs of physical illness. Old people and the jobless also make demands in excess of the demands of the young and employed. Their behaviour may seem abnormal when there is any neglect. The reason for neglect is that they are no longer useful (productively abnormal).

3. *Over-playing a part:* The passive, non-aggressive person (normal) who is so passive (abnormal) that he is quite incapable of making any kind of decision and is extremely dependent. A person who, through fear of rejection, over-conforms (i.e. passively follows others) loses his "no" feeling which is his capa-

city for growth. There is aggression in over-conforming; passivity should not be thought of as always non-aggressive. At the other extreme is the active and enterprising person (normal) who becomes intolerant of criticism and fearful of dependence (abnormal). In politics this can lead to dictatorship with its ruthless suppression of any opposition.

An interesting example of over-conforming was provided by some research carried out among a group of trainee soldiers in the U.S. Army.

One thinks of a soldier as someone who will unhesitatingly obey commands. It has been said, for instance, that a soldier in a crack regiment would march over the side of a cliff if he wasn't given the command to halt. But a soldier must also show initiative. In the heat of battle there may not be anyone around to give orders.

The study of the soldiers who over-conformed (or were "over-automated" as a psychologist friend of mine suggested) revealed that most of them had records of job failure, school truancy and other minor difficulties in their home-town communities before they joined the Army. On joining up they were anxious to turn over a new leaf, to show that they were capable of good behaviour. They went to such lengths to please their superior officers that they were capable of scrubbing a floor until their fingers bled. What this type of soldier didn't understand was that "regulation" reality is different from the reality of group life : i.e. the way soldiers interact with one another in groups. All the drilling is forgotten in the mess when soldiers are no different from civilians except that they wear uniforms; their behaviour is similar to the behaviour of other groups outside the Army. For example, there are certain "cues" for initiating interaction in a group—e.g. asking for matches or offering a cigarette to start a conversation—and there are usually "in-jokes" about people and life in a group and also "in-words" : i.e. words that have a special meaning within the group. There are a hundred and one different ways in which members of a group develop a style which everyone adopts.

The over-conforming soldier in the American study was a caricature of the group style. For instance, the case is cited of a soldier who gave away cigarettes. One of his fellow-soldiers said : "I was out of cigarettes and he had a whole pack. I said, 'Joe, you got a smoke?' He says, 'Yes', and Jesus, he gave me about twelve of them. At other times he used to offer me two or three packs of cigarettes at a time when I was out."

There are also ways in which people greet one another. The trainee in the study picked up these forms of greeting, but used them repeatedly on inappropriate occasions . . . "He'd go by you in the barracks and say, 'What do you say, Jake?' I'd say, 'Hi, George, how are you?' and he'd walk into the latrine. And he'd come by not a minute later, and it's the same thing all over again, 'What do you say, Jake?' It seemed to me he was always saying 'Hi' to someone. You could be sitting right beside him for ten minutes and he would keep on saying it."

There are young people like these soldiers with records of bad behaviour at school who, on going into industry or business, seem odd because of their anxiety to please; they suppress their natural feelings of aggression. They cannot say "No" any more because in the past they may perhaps have said "No" to everything. When to say "No" in a way that doesn't offend is one of the most important lessons we can learn in life. There is a school for maladjusted boys where the cook is said to be able to say "No" with all the atmosphere of saying "Yes". This is a rare ability, even among school teachers or psychotherapists.

4. *Misdirected intelligence or creativity:* The same degree of creative energy sometimes goes into the planning of a crime as into worthwhile activities. The planning of the Great Train Robbery, for instance, was an example of misdirected intelligence.

The misuse of a good brain is also illustrated in the tragic case of Nathan Leopold, one of the two youths who "murdered for thrills" in the 1920s, plotting "the perfect crime," which resulted in the killing of a fifteen-year-old boy. Leopold was sentenced to life imprisonment. After serving thirty-three years of his sentence he was released from jail and shortly afterwards set up a foundation to aid emotionally disturbed, retarded and delinquent youths. He obtained a master's degree in social work and became a senior officer of the Puerto Rican Department of Health. It was reported after his death that his brain would be removed and studied for clues to its capacity for genius.

It is interesting that in a research project that examined the criminal characteristics of fifty delinquent boys of superior intelligence, compared with a group of delinquents of average intelligence, it was found that more high-I-Q boys committed offences which seemed to be psychologically determined—i.e. their crimes could not be explained in terms of the influence of a delinquent environment. The most serious offence was committed by a bright boy who stabbed his own father.

How many young people are there today, one wonders, who like Leopold have first-class brains that could be used in some worthwhile occupation, but are misused in criminal activities? The recent reforms in the law that allow judges to offer social work as an alternative to jail sentences or fines may save some of these youngsters from a life of crime.

5. *People who opt out: Tramps; Hippies.*

What do you do with people who opt out? Let me quote the case of Joan who, neglected by her parents, ran away from home and went to live with a group of Hippies. She did nothing useful and was always getting into trouble. Her way back to living a useful life was via the Henderson Hospital in Sutton, Surrey, where patients like Joan are allowed to be what they want to be, but only on certain conditions. They are told that they must examine those freedoms in themselves that lead them to behave aggressively. They do this together in groups; but it is tough going. They have to become transparent, exposing all their thoughts and ideas and feelings.

"To begin with it was quite a hard graft," Joan said. "For the first three months I couldn't really think what I was doing there; I just couldn't seem to work out where I was. But you just have to talk, rip yourself open."

Joan talked about "acting out" her aggression, which in her case meant breaking windows and milk bottles. At the Henderson this kind of behaviour is not considered unreasonable for someone with Joan's background; but one of the conditions for remaining there is, as Joan put it, "you've got to have an explanation."

"What else could I do?" might be an explanation. "It's better to smash a milk bottle than somebody's head." But I suspect the real explanation is : "Nobody's taught me to use my aggression in a constructive way because until I came here I've been told I'm no good—and that's all there is to be said. I have no skills; I'm useless." And this probably is the explanation for a great deal of the aggression in society today.

There are, in my opinion, seven basic freedoms which, if denied, will lead to aggression. They are :

1. *Being.* Freedom to be yourself, which means feeling secure enough to be honest about yourself.
2. *Thinking.* Freedom to ask questions, to reject what others say you should think, to learn through direct experience, to be allowed to make mistakes without feeling a failure.
3. *Loving.* Freedom to love, to express your love in any way you choose so long as you are seeking real relationships with others and you are not exploiting others or using them for your own ends.
4. *Praying.* Freedom to worship, at least to spend a part of your day, wherever you happen to be, in meditation or prayer without interference. Time and space must be set aside for this purpose.
5. *Retreating.* Freedom to retreat to a position where you can lick your wounds and regain strength.
6. *Playing.* Freedom to play for no reason at all except for the pleasure of feeling alive.
7. *Working.* Freedom to do work in which all your talents are used, which means sharing in the drudgery of others so that they too can do work that will give them a feeling of self-fulfilment.

14

The Alternative Society

Remember that all the advice given by grown-up
people to young people has interested motives,
and that the world belongs to the rebellious.
—Bernard Shaw : from a letter to
a seventeen-year-old girl, 1900.

THERE are young people who talk of overthrowing the Establishment by means of "Play Power."

"Why work?" they say. "There's no virtue in work for its own sake. Have fun. Why wear yourself out in some dull job so that you can go home to your telly or have a few drinks at the local or keep up the payments on the mortgage or have your two or three weeks holiday at Margate or on the Costa Brava? This is using up your life—or most of it—without pleasure. The whole of life should be a holiday. Work should be enjoyable. Education should be fun. Work and fun should not be two separate things."

Richard Neville, in his book called *Playpower*, says purposeless play is creative. The most inventive scientists and researchers play. Many new inventions started out as toys. Artists play. Why? Because purposeless play is "affirmation of life"—not an attempt to bring order out of chaos, nor to suggest improvements in creation, but "simply a way of waking up to the very life we're living, which is so excellent once one gets one's mind and one's desires out of the way and lets it act of its own accord. You should go around making friends with people. Say hello to strangers. Nobody ever does."

Neville also mentions the fun a group of youngsters had in Selfridges one Christmas. They stepped into the department store with one of them dressed as Santa Claus and gave away "free presents" to surprised customers, who probably wondered what the "catch" was. But there wasn't a catch. Christmas, everybody agrees, has become a commercial bonanza.

The youngsters were protesting about this by showing people what Christmas should mean—a season of goodwill.

The philosopher, Herbert Marcuse, also calls for "the convergence of work and play." The creative imagination should be applied to all those things we do that we call work. A man's usefulness should not be measured merely by his performance at work—i.e. the profitability of what he does. More important is his creativity. The creative imagination should become a "productive force."

To draw attention to what they consider the false values of present-day society young people sometimes stage what they call "happenings." A happening is something that calls for the spontaneous participation of everybody. At the theatre the audience are part of the performance; there is no sharp division between actors and audience. In this way we become aware of ourselves. We become fully conscious. Most of us do not experience this sense of reality except in an emergency in wartime when we are in extreme danger, or when there is a death or serious illness in the family. At such times our faculty of observation is enhanced. A "happening" is an attempt to create this state of enhanced observation : not in a contrived, but in a spontaneous way. The unexpected makes everyone sit up and take notice.

Not so easy to explain is the more threatening behaviour of activist groups, especially in the States and on the Continent. For instance, many found the behaviour of a group of young German students, who called themselves Kommune 1, very puzzling. They distributed leaflets which suggested—Richard Neville said "philosophically"—that, in protest against the horrors of Vietnam, fires should be started in various buildings in Berlin, including two American buildings. These buildings were to be set on fire while they were occupied.

Kommune 1 was formed in 1967 primarily, as they said, to free themselves from "bourgeois values." But they argued, if you as an individual succeed in changing yourself, you owe it to your fellow-men to take action to change their rotten world. "If you want to be a human being," they said, "you have to over-throw the system. Refuse to put up with the rules of a bureau-cratic society." They quoted Che Guevara: "It is the men of the twenty-first century we have to create."

Because many young people feel a burning desire to "smash the pigeon holes" of present day society they talk much about the need for revolution. One good answer to this was given by those popular figures John Lennon and Paul McCartney:

> You say you want a revolution.
> Well you know
> we all want to change the world.
> You tell me that it's evolution.
> Well you know
> we all want to change the world.
> But when you talk about destruction
> Don't you know that you can count me out.
> Don't you know it's gonna be all right.
> All right.   All right.

The revolution that many intelligent young people are talking and writing about is not, however, a violent one, but a moral revolution. They see the need, as many of us do now, I hope, of changing our directions so that, for instance, the very young and the very old are not neglected and also those who break the law, particularly young offenders, do not end up in a social pocket from which there is no return.

Their "alternatives" include RAP (Radical Alternatives to Prison) who argue that putting people behind bars for breaking the law is not only expensive and counter-productive, but also immoral. "While old people die of cold," they say, "who can get excited about a mother of six shoplifting?" Nobody goes to prison when an old person dies of cold or when a child is killed on the road because he has nowhere to play. We are too much concerned, say members of RAP, with locking people up. Many people who end up with ten-year-plus sentences claim that it all started in approved school, that they were sent away—for "training"—as a harmless pilferer, and learned so much about crime that they emerged with higher ambitions.

Young people hate the twentieth century city with its paving stones and glass and concrete. But let them speak for themselves:

"As I look, or think of modern society, an image of clinical plastic concrete vastness overcomes me and I am scared. This may well sound immature but the truth is that the future for me, and certainly for my children, seems the most frightening aspect of my life. I cannot bear to think of overcrowding, the loss of the countryside, and all the things which Ecology is shouting at us the whole time. Yet how helpless we are—of course."

girl, Southern England

"The fact that people are becoming less and less identifiable worries me. You walk through a London street and it's so impersonal, it makes you feel really cold."

boy, Southern England

"Many people are losing their individuality these days—they're being classified like plants and animals. This gives people a complex about themselves, as they feel that they are just one of the nameless mass or just 'you'. These 'yous' are getting shut up in boxes, cut off from the rest."

girl, North

"The most worrying thing about modern society is the completely impersonal attitude to people that is taken. There are too many machines, and not enough people taking the trouble to find out about others. Most people seem to have numbers given to them, in either their banking account or their insurance policy. Nobody is known by their name any more and if society is not careful people will become so wrapped up in themselves that they will not be able to see pain and suffering in others."

girl, South Midlands

"The thing that worries me is that I'll turn out to be *moderate* —I don't like doing things moderately, and the fact that I might turn into a moderate architect with an ordinary wife and an ordinary suburban home distresses me."

boy, North Midlands

"My main hope is that I will not ignore people who are suffering and treat them as part of the landscape. I hope I don't become selfish in striving to do what I want. I want to be devoted to doing social work as well as being devoted to a life in sport : two things which are very difficult to do at the same time. I don't want to get involved in the rat race for money. I hope to see society in a considerably better state than it is in now due to an outright and firm attempt, by the more fortunate people in this day and age, to help and love those who are suffering. I don't want to become a machine, doing exactly the same as everybody else, and in so doing finding myself ignoring people."

boy, South Midlands

"In the West, we're rich, too rich. But we're like some great rich Christmas pudding with a decaying rotten core, and black burnt currants, with nice cream to disguise it all. I think I could probably accept moderate well-being and material comfort if everyone shared it, and had likewise. I see pictures of places like Bengal, and I think, 'How awful. I wish I could do something,' but I forget. It seems so stupid, man with all his power has rockets and starvation existing side by side."

girl, South Midlands

When we are young we are very impressionable, and we also want to make an impression. We try very hard to make ourselves felt, but often all the young person sees is a series of demands made on him at home and school—in fact, all the way through life from childhood.

Fifteen-year-old Mary, whom I met at a Richmond Fellowship hostel in Southampton, put it very succinctly : "My mother doesn't show any affection. She's very intellectual. Everything to her is O-levels, A-levels and a degree. And that's it. I've disappointed her greatly."

Mary found the situation at home one she had to get away from to be able to see things clearly. "There's so much mis-understanding between the generations. The older generation should help us more. . . . Young people are crying out for peace in the world and understanding. The older generation stick up a huge barrier of prejudice. There's no contact—just a great big empty space."

Mary was made to feel inadequate because her mother had cast her in a superior role. She is much happier now where nobody expects her to be anyone else but herself.

A reaction to a sense of frustration is not only responsible for inner tensions, but possibly for much of the violence in our society. Research into the causes of delinquency has shown that a feeling of helplessness—the individual deeply believing that he can neither change nor influence anything, especially his life course—is a major cause of aggressive behaviour. Similarly aggression between a husband and wife is often caused by a sense of frustration in sexual relationships.

It is somebody else's theory and the rigidity with which it is applied about "good" behaviour, the need for discipline, the need for spontaneity, the meaning of success, how to be successful, how to bring up children, and so on, that often makes things go wrong. Somebody's theory, in fact, may later become every-body's reality—or nightmare.

Our first environment is the womb; and while we are still there our life-style is being decided for us by the expectations of parents. When, for example, parents say they would like a boy, they are thinking of the male role in life, which brings greater material rewards than the female role, and consequently they do not really want a child, but a man. They see the child as grown-up even before it is born; and in some of the ways we educate our children we are treating them as little adults, projecting them into the future instead of allowing them to live in and enjoy the present. We are taking the present away from them.

All sorts of people, mostly the young, are distributing pamphlets, putting stickers everywhere and marching around with banners proclaiming that they have the solutions to the world's problems. There is nothing new about this, of course. I remember myself, during the thirties, joining a march led by Donald Soper (now Lord Soper) in the West End of London. I carried a banner on which were the words "I refuse to fight." We were all pacifists then. We believed that if we could get enough people to refuse to fight there would not be another war. But it took an atom bomb to convince people that war was criminal and solved nothing.

The present generation, when it becomes the older generation, will find that they too have made mistakes. And the worst mistake, I believe, one can make is to become too rigid in one's beliefs. Young people are right when they urge this need for flexibility if they are to enjoy the "good life," perhaps best described as "the integration of action, enjoyment and contemplation."

15

Opinions and Definitions

THROUGHOUT history there have been attempts to make people fit into categories. An ancient Chinese book, I Ching : the Book of Changes, which inspired some of the profoundest aphorisms of Lao-tse and Confucius, and which Jung thought so highly of, describes the world of being as the interplay between the firm and the yielding, qualities which in people appear as creative (representing the nature of heaven : "active, strong—of the spirit") and receptive (the nature of earth : "complementing the creative—strong in devotion").

Hippocrates placed people into four main categories according to their temperaments : choleric, sanguine, melancholic and phlegmatic, symbolised by the four elements :

Choleric: fire, warm and dry, quick and strong

Sanguine: air, warm and moist, slow and weak

Melancholic: earth, cold and dry, slow and strong

Phlegmatic: water, cold and moist, slow and calm

This theory of Hippocrates, of almost 2,500 years ago, has in it, according to psychologist H. J. Eysenck, a strong element of truth. Eysenck has made use of it in defining categories of personality established as the result of extensive laboratory tests. But for the most part all that remains of Hippocrates' categories are their negative aspects—e.g. choleric now means easily angered.

Carl Jung described people as falling into two main categories —introverts and extraverts. The introvert is not very sociable, prefers working alone, but is not necessarily withdrawn. He may be a studious person with a great deal of charm, an easy, quiet manner in company—modest but self-assured. The extravert is the "hail fellow well met" type; he may be boisterous and empty-headed, but he could be an alert, friendly person with qualities of leadership.

Jung's distinction of introverts and extraverts was later refined into endomorphs, mesomorphs and ectomorphs. The predominantly endormorphic type is sociable, fat and jolly, fond of eating and drinking; he usually has a paunch. The predominantly mesomorphic type is a muscleman (beefy); he is energetic and likes exercise; physically he has wide shoulders and narrow hips. The predominantly ectomorphic type is sensitive, dislikes company and is the sort of person whom the "underground" might describe as "uptight." Physically he tends to be thin, with drooping shoulders.

In his psychological laboratory, Eysenck claims to have established a connection between the behaviour of introverts and extraverts with the "reticular formation"* in the brain stem, which he says processes the input of sensual information in a way that inhibits or excites cervical activity. Eysenck worked out a scientific procedure for grading introverts and extraverts. The way he did this is too complicated to explain here, but briefly he set a subject a rather monotonous, mechanical task to do, and kept him at it, but allowing rest periods at regular intervals. He found that the performance of his subjects varied after the rest period and that involuntary rest periods were taken, more frequently by some than others.

* If Eysenck's theory about the "reticular formation" is correct, it would appear that introversion and extraversion are inherited qualities. There are others, however, who believe that these qualities develop in childhood as a result of parental attitudes. Sheldon and Eleanor Glueck, of the Harvard Law School, found that predominantly extravert boys were more likely to be reared by emotionally healthy than unhealthy mothers. Extraversion in boys, they found, was associated with an affectionate father or with a father who took the lead in the home. Extravert children were also more likely to be found in homes where their playmates were welcomed and introvert children where parents were inhospitable.

The conclusions he came to were interesting. The extravert he discovered was, surprisingly, easily inhibited in the sense that he soon became bored and was unable to concentrate for long periods. His performance did not improve after a rest period as it did with the introvert, because of lack of what he calls the "reminiscence" phenomenon—i.e. the ability to do better after a rest without further practice. What this showed was that the extravert needed more stimulation than the introvert; he was no good at work of the purely mechanical kind; he needed variety.

The introvert, on the other hand, did not take as many involuntary rest periods as the extravert and came back after a rest to show improved performance. What this demonstrated was the greater staying power of the introvert; he took infinite care over whatever he was doing; he was possibly inspired but always diligent. Too much stimulation disturbed him.

Eysenck classifies extraverts and introverts according to grades of stability and instability which shade into one another. The unstable extravert he describes as having the negative aspects of the Hippocratic choleric temperament—i.e. touchy, restless, aggressive; the stable extravert has the positive qualities of the sanguine temperament—i.e. sociable, outgoing, responsive. The unstable introvert is moody, anxious, unsociable (the melancholic temperament); the stable introvert is thoughtful, reliable, even-tempered (phlegmatic).

This is useful information and forms the basis of personality tests sometimes used to grade a person in industry and commerce and in career counselling. "Square pegs in round holes" are people who are temperamentally unsuited to the kind of work they have to do (introverts doing an extravert's job and *vice versa*) and this usually results in a great deal of anxiety.

Eysenck maintains that it is possible to control behaviour by means of drugs which shift a person's position in the extra-version/introversion continuum. An aggressive extravert, for example, would—perhaps surprisingly—be treated with a stimulant drug. The extravert, needing stimulation and not getting enough of it, may become aggressive. The stimulant drug has the effect of speeding up brain activity, producing a pleasurable sensation that makes it unnecessary for the unstable extravert to seek his stimulation in aggressive behaviour. The introvert, on the other hand, would be given a depressant drug, with the same properties as alcohol, which is not, as some believe, a stimulant but an inhibitory drug : it slows down brain activity.

One can see, therefore, that an introvert who has to work in a way that does not suit his temperament might seek relief in alcohol which has the effect of turning him into an extravert. Thus, possibly, the majority of people who frequent pubs are not predominantly extraverts, but unstable introverts. The extraverts, needing variety, would not like wasting time in a pub. An unstable extravert, however, might become hooked on a stimulant drug, such as methedrine.

The young, slap-happy, devil-may-care hooligan who rips train seats and gets involved in brawls is obviously an unstable extravert or has become one as the result of alcohol or drug abuse. There is ample evidence that criminal types are more predominantly extraverts than introverts—these are usually law-abiding, socially conforming individuals and are better subjects for "conditioning" than extraverts.

A number of studies are cited by psychologists to confirm the extravert theory of criminality, including some research with a group of particularly aggressive inmates of Joliet Penitentiary in Chicago, all of whom were found to be highly extraverted.

There are other factors involved, of course : psychological, biological, moral or cultural—not only one cause but usually a combination of different causes; each individual in his orientation is unique. But one can probably say that the unstable extravert tends to turn his aggression outwards, whilst the neurotic, over-inhibited introvert turns his aggression inwards. The unstable extravert hurts others or damages property; the unstable introvert hurts himself, or if he hurts others it will probably be in a furtive way or in a sudden discharge of feelings which he has bottled up over a period of time ... "Beware the fury of a patient man." There are many instances of the Crippen-type murderer, the mild, inhibited man who suddenly kills.

A classic example of a man who saved his rage and resentment until the pressure became unbearable is given by Dr. Hans Toch in a recent book called "Violent Men." Dr. Toch is Professor of Psychology in the School of Criminal Justice at the State University of New York. In his book he cites the case of a wife killer—called Jim for the purposes of his account. The man Jim arrived home one day to find his wife in bed with a neighbouring farmer. He was shocked and unhappy, but managed to hide his feelings; he merely closed the door and went into a field to cry. He knew that there was a loaded rifle in the room next to the bedroom and any other man might have grabbed it in a fury. But not Jim. To his wife and her lover he did not appear to be unduly perturbed. His behaviour was therefore taken by his wife to indicate that he had no objection to her infidelity, so she went on going to bed with the other man and even invited him to meals whenever he came to stay overnight.

This arrangement continued for three years and Jim never complained. One day Jim returned home to be told that the other man had left with his wife and children and all the furniture and livestock, which he had loaded into one of Jim's trucks. Jim took all this very calmly, or so it seemed, and made no attempt to bring his wife back.

Eventually Jim married again. And then almost the same thing happened. His wife acquired a lover. This wife, like the previous one, was a domineering woman who subjected Jim to an endless series of demands. But when she took a lover Jim could no longer hold back his rage and he murdered her in a very brutal way. Koch comments that the second wife inherited "the suppressed resentment of Jim's past," and he makes the point that there are people who submit to another person's unreasonable demands, but after a time, unable to cope any longer, they respond with blind and senseless rage, usually directed at others, and then "revert to a state of forced, tortured passivity."

Koch's research shows that people with emotional problems can best help themselves by helping others with similar problems. By discussing their problems together they gain insights into why they are violent. This sort of thing happens at the Richmond Fellowship hostels and at meetings of Alcoholics Anonymous. "Groups of violent men," says Koch, "given the task of re-educating each other, could do this by reinforcing each other's strengths, by helping each other in joint activities, and by each analysing the others' roles in the enterprises of their community."

The conclusion Koch came to after interviewing seventy-five violent-prone prisoners can be summed up in one sentence—if one has respect for oneself as a person there can be no violence. Violence (or for that matter, any kind of aggressive behaviour) occurs when one feels the need to defend one's reputation or self-image or to promote (even when there is no incitement to violence or aggression) a self-definition of toughness; or to defend oneself (as a result of low self-esteem) against some imagined slight or threat; or to remove pressure from some explosive situation in which one is unable to cope, largely as a result of limited social skills.

Violence or aggression also occurs as the result of a sadistic impulse (bullying) to injure others who are uniquely susceptible to it; to manipuate others (exploitation) into becoming unwilling tools of one's pleasure or convenience; or as the result of a tendency to operate under the assumption that other people exist to satisfy one's needs (self-indulging); or to discharge accumulated internal pressure (catharting).

Here we must also consider the views which have been expressed about behaviourism—a psychological approach which explains all behaviour in terms of conditioning. According to this theory a human being can be likened to a highly complicated machine or computer programmed to perform some useful social function. He or she is merely the product of his environment and can be conditioned, by means of drugs or behaviour therapy —reward and punishment—to behave as we want him to. It is simply a matter of understanding how the machine works.

Adjustment becomes a virtue, and the morality of one's actions is judged according to their social usefulness.

Many young people stay aloof from their families or leave home altogether. They neglect the social amenities; they are poorly dressed, dirty and rude. They take time off from school or the university.... And so on. What, one may ask, is to be done about it? By strengthening, say the behavioural psychologists, "the contingencies of reinforcement," by which they mean the conditions in which a person feels that what he is doing is satisfying and rewarding. Thus the questions we should be asking about the "drop-out," or the shiftless, dull youth, are "How reinforcing is the place in which he works? Or, how do his supervisors and fellow workers treat him?"

People are, of course, to a fairly large extent the products of their environment. Conditioning goes on from the moment a person is born; often we are unconscious of it. We see conditioning working in the supermarket and the motor showroom. People are constantly being persuaded to buy things they do not really want or need through clever advertising and public relations—the manipulation game.

There is somebody's cosmetic to give you "a pure, fresh, natural beauty;" a drink in a bottle claimed to be "the most natural taste under the sun"—and it's not milk! "It's natural..." introduces an advertisement for a cigarette that may give someone cancer. There are cars for "getaway people." But where do they get away to?

There is a growing fear that because of sophisticated techniques in manipulation we shall soon have the sort of society described by George Orwell in 1984. Some say it is already here. Young people see the dangers more than the older generation. Timothy Leary (not a young man, but one of the prophets of the permissive society) wrote—"I am a mind... a box of conditioned Pavlovian reflexes, a social robot, here adjusted, there maladjusted, sometimes good (approved of), sometimes bad (censored). The centre of my psychological mandala, the mainspring of my personality, is social conditioning... what will the neighbour think? is the beginning and end of modern psychology."

The point missed by some critics of the film *The Clockwork Orange*, which, understandably, many objected to for its horrifying scenes of violence, is that freedom of action, in which there are risks, is better than meek obedience.

The film is relevant to this book, and for those who did not see it the story is of an unruly and violent young man who is treated and "cured" by means of aversion therapy, which, however, produces a completely negative personality. He becomes just an empty shell. One of the things that happens as the result of conditioning is that the boy no longer finds pleasure, as he did before the treatment, in a Beethoven symphony. For him Beethoven meant violence.

To demonstrate the effectiveness of the treatment to a gathering of experts, he is made to lick the sole of somebody's boot. He becomes less than human, submissive and grovelling. At least there was some hope for him whilst he continued to enjoy Beethoven. The end of the film is his de-conditioning— and one breathes a sigh of relief.

The problem is how far does one go in imposing patterns of behaviour through external manipulation? And who does the manipulating? "The possibilities of altering a person's behaviour," says Dr. Peter Schiller, a psychiatrist in private practice in London, "are immense, but the way in which they are used can be determined only by the degree of maturity and morality within the society which has access to them. Psychiatry in the future will be limited not so much by what is possible, as by what is morally permissible."

Erich Fromm complains that the emphasis in modern psychology is on "adjustment" rather than "goodness" and he does not see how one can possibly divorce problems of ethics from the study of personality. "The value of judgments we make," he says, "determine our actions, and upon their validity rests our mental health and happiness. To consider evaluations as so many rationalisations of unconscious, irrational desires—

although they can be that too—narrows down and distorts our picture of the total personality. Neurosis itself is, in the last analysis, a symptom of moral failure (although 'adjustment' is by no means a symptom of moral achievement). In many instances a neurotic symptom is the specific expression of moral conflict, and the success of the therapeutic effort depends on the understanding and solution of the person's moral problem."

Describing conscience as "man's recall to himself" he says that it is not an internalized voice of an authority, but our own voice, "present in every human being and independent of external sanctions and rewards. . . . Conscience judges our functioning as human beings; it is (as the root of the word *conscientia* indicates) knowledge *within* oneself, knowledge of our respective success or failure in the art of living. . . . Actions, thoughts and feelings which are conducive to the proper functioning and unfolding of our total personality produce a feeling of inner approval, of 'rightness' . . ."

Abraham Maslow differentiates between intrinsic conscience and intrinsic guilt. The former he describes as the taking into the self of the disapprovals and approvals of persons other than the person himself, fathers, mothers, teachers, etc. Guilt then is recognition of disapproval by others. Intrinsic guilt, on the other hand, is the betrayal of one's own inner nature or self. Maslow sees intrinsic guilt as an inner guide for growth.

It is not enough to know if someone is an extravert or introvert, stable or otherwise. It does not, in fact, tell us very much at all. What we really need to know is not that someone is reliable or sociable—you can get personalities who would qualify according to their own standards, as "reliable" or "sociable" in a teenage gang—but what is much more important are the standards by which one lives, one's moral and cultural beliefs. Eysenck, whom I have quoted earlier in this chapter, like all behaviourists, makes the mistake of confusing behaviour with character. As Fromm points out, a man can *behave* in a courageous way for the wrong motives. A man who is ambitious, for example, may risk his life to satisfy his craving to be admired.

Nor does the behaviourist pay a great deal of regard to the individual as he sees himself, often feeling vulnerable and guilty, but believing in his own uniqueness—

that I am I is only mine and belongs to me and to nobody else.

"Our moral problem is man's indifference to himself," said Fromm. From the psychological viewpoint, he maintains, the most crucial problem today is man's attitude to force and power. "Physical force can deprive us of our freedom and kill us. Whether we can resist or overcome it depends on the accidental factors of our own physical strength and the strength of our weapons. Our mind, on the other hand, is not directly subject to power. The truth which we have recognised, the ideas in which we have faith, do not become invalidated by force. Might and reason exist on different planes and force never disproves truth." In the moral dilemma we find ourselves in today "neither the good nor the evil outcome is automatic or preordained. The decision rests with man. It rests upon his ability to take himself, his life and happiness seriously; on his willingness to face his society's moral problem. It rests upon his courage to be himself and to be for himself."

Fromm criticises Freud for coming too much under the influence of the Darwinian concepts of his epoch with the result that he failed to see the vital difference between animal behaviour, in which the animal always follows its instincts and human behaviour, in which man is relatively free to follow his drives or not.

"Freud's concept of sex is that of an urge springing entirely from physiologically conditioned tension, relieved, like hunger, by satisfaction . . ." He ignores man's freedom to seek his own happiness, including his sexual *desire*—not his *need*. "Happiness . . . is not a need springing from a physiological or psychological lack; it is not the relief from tension but the accompaniment of all productive activity in thought, feeling, and action."

While Freud explained people's troubles in terms of sexual

cause, Alfred Adler, the Austrian psychiatrist, did so in terms of a power urge. The key to all social progress, Adler declared, was to be found in the fact that individuals were always looking for situations in which they excelled. His Swiss contemporary Jung sought an explanation in the *complexes* which he described as clusters of ideas formed by experience or by the way the individual reacts to experience; these complexes sometimes surge into the conscious mind in an uncontrollable way. Of the three Jung seems to have the most appeal for young people today, partly because of his interest in the occult and in Eastern religions with which many young people are now trying to identify.

Jung's psychology verges on mysticism. His belief in the balancing function of opposites recalls the *yin* and *yang* of Taoism—"the positive and negative principles which, in dynamic balance, maintain the order of the world." Jung believed that a person who clearly sees the evil in himself allows the good to come to surface. By recognising and confronting the negative aspects of consciousness the positive aspects are thrown up.

The Shadow was the name Jung gave to his conception of the unconscious, which embraced the *personal unconscious,* formed from repressed infantile wishes and impulses and from many other forgotten experiences, and the *collective unconscious* "the whole historical aspect of the unconscious"—which Jung described as a deep stratum of the unconscious that is common to all mankind and "goes back into the realm of our animal ancestors."

Sometimes the unconscious, says Jung, makes us behave in ways that are morally reprehensible. The irrational forces that go back to our animal ancestry may become a positive danger to ourselves and to the community. These forces can break out in irrational wars which nobody wants, or in revolutions. In personal life these forces often produce periods of libertinism, unrestraint and gangsterism. In industry they spark off unrest and strikes.

The influence of the "unknown" is seen operating in the way

a child is disturbed by parental difficulties even when there is a careful attempt to conceal them. "Not in front of the children" should never be said; if there is something of an emotional nature to conceal, the child will know it, so it is better to come out into the open with it.

We now know more about how a child becomes aware of these feelings. The true feelings of a parent cannot be covered up in a smiling face. There are other signals—paralinguistic signals—"ers" and "ums" or a false tone of voice—and non-verbal signals, such as a nervous gesture of the hands, an exchange of glances between parents and other signs of anxiety that a child quickly—and correctly—interprets.

There are many who believe that we are born with an aggressive instinct, as necessary as sex in the preservation and propagation of the species; and, like the sexual impulse, they say it must find an outlet. Illness and deviant behaviour according to them, are very often caused by the bottling up of innate aggressive feelings.

The study of animal behaviour, particularly of ritualised behaviour including so-called appeasing attitudes, show certain similarities with human behaviour and seem to point to the presence of a potentially dangerous and destructive element in human nature. Aggressive behaviour in the animal kingdom is associated with the animals' need to have to protect their home or land or food supply and their offspring; and, secondly, the establishment of dominance in a social hierarchy.

Some animals that do not live in groups are purely territorial and obviously have no hierarchy problems. Others that roam about in groups have no territorial problems and are purely hierarchical. There is a rigidly established social hierarchy (which is sometimes referred to as "the pecking order" because it was first noticed among chickens) in most species of monkeys and apes, with a dominant male at the head of the group, and others ranged below him in varying degrees of subordination. Desmond Morris in his best-seller *The Naked Ape* explains what happens when the leader becomes too weak and old to maintain his dominance: "He is overthrown by a younger, sturdier male, who then assumes the mantle of the colony boss. (In some cases the usurper literally assumes the mantle, growing one in the form of a cape of long hair.) As the troop keeps together all the time, his role as group tyrant is incessantly operative. But despite this he is invariably the sleekest, best-groomed and sexiest monkey in the community."

Human beings have both territorial and hierarchical problems. One can see the former operating in wars in defence of a country or in the conquest of new territories for economic benefits; and in the importance attached to private property and the aggressive feelings every individual has when there is any invasion of his privacy. Nothing seems so menacing as a stranger who trespasses on our land or who enters our home uninvited; and the law upholds the individual's right to protect his property against intruders. Even the police are not allowed on one's land or in one's home without a search warrant.

A man needs space around him, and one of the reasons why there is so much aggression in our cities is that individuals do not always get the space they need. There is overcrowding; people feel threatened and unhappy when this happens and, if they can afford it, go dashing out into the country—to the "wide open spaces"—whenever they are presented with the opportunity. There is probably an enormous amount of repressed aggression in crowded tubes during the rush hour.

The need for space probably originated in the necessity for animals to organise their habitat so that each can secure its share of the available food supply. It is not, however, for food that most of us need space today, but for the sense of freedom it gives us, and also for hierarchical reasons.

In our cities quality rather than quantity is important. A Mayfair flat may be smaller than many a suburban house, but it gives its occupant a superior status. Hierarchical considerations work in the opposite way in offices. The boss has the largest amount of space around him: he is more isolated than anyone else and sometimes has an adjoining office—a buffer zone—for his secretary to keep intruders out. The higher in the hierarchy, the more space a man is entitled to; the lower, the less space. The least paid workers are given very little space in which to operate, and if they are cleaners and floor sweepers they are given no space at all, and move around invading the space of others, who, though polite—usually over-polite—are glad when the intruders move out. The space we occupy plays a very important part in human relationships .

Dr. A. F. Kinzel, of the New York Psychiatric Institute, carried out some experiments with inmates of the U.S. Medical Center for Federal Prisoners, which seemed to show that the most violent men were those who needed the most space around them. Some of them preferred solitary confinement with all its deprivations so that they could have space of their own away from other inmates. When these men were violent in prison they usually explained that it was because other prisoners were "messing about with me" or "getting up in my face" but it was generally found that what had actually happened was that their victims had come too close to them.

What precisely too close meant was the object of Dr. Kinzel's experiment. He took fifteen volunteers, eight of them with violent histories and a control group of seven who were not violent, and approached each prisoner in turn asking him to indicate when he felt that he was coming too close for their comfort. The result of the experiment was that Kinzel found those with violent histories needed twice the space (body buffer zone) as the others. The lesson of this experiment is that it explains perhaps why violence occurs in overcrowded slums or in families where everyone is "on top of one another" and where there are no open spaces for people to play in or relax.

Overcrowding is undoubtedly a breeding ground of hostility. We all need space in which to operate; although how large this space might be for each human being, for each family, is a matter to which little thought has been accorded. It is becoming more urgent as population increases. Modern medicine and hygiene have so decreased the death rate that, every day, twice as many people are born as die ... every year the world has sixty-three million new mouths to feed.

Dr. J. B. Calhoun, chief of the behavioural systems section at the United States National Institute of Health, created what he called "a mouse universe", with space and food supply remaining the same while the population increased. He claimed that the experiment showed how a species could die out. He provided enough food for 9,500 mice, enough water for 6,000 and yet when the population reached about 2,200, large pools of outcast mice had grown up and the females had become aggressive and turned on their young. The mice eventually stopped breeding and Dr. Calhoun was left with 180 elderly animals all aged over eighty in human terms. The mice ceased to take part in the normal interaction of mouse society and became autistic and self-centred.

The same thing, he believed, could happen with man. "By my calculation, this could happen in 1985 or 1986, but 1984 has a better ring to it."

It is, of course, ridiculous to make predictions of this sort based on the behaviour of mice. But even so, there is cause for alarm at the way the population is increasing. Over-population and pollution are matters of grave concern, especially to the young people who will inherit the future but see their world being gradually destroyed by the greed and indifference of the older generation. It is the older generation, they say, who are aggressive and do often excuse themselves by saying that you can't change human nature.

It may be comforting, but it is a denial of our human dignity to shift the responsibility for all the aggression and violence in society on to our "innate aggressiveness." The whole argument about whether aggression is an instinct or not was dismissed by G. K. Chesterton years ago when he said, "There is no more an instinct of cruelty than there is an instinct of chewing glass."

16

A School Doctor's View

by

Ronald Gibson, C.B.E., M.A., LL.D., F.R.C.S., is a General Practitioner and a Medical Officer to Winchester College and St. Swithun's School Winchester.

Let me first give you four quotations.

Firstly: "Our youth loves luxury, has bad manners, disregards authority and has no respect whatsoever for age; our today's children are tyrants; they do not get up when an elderly man enters the room—they talk back to their parents—they are just very bad."

Secondly: "I have no longer any hope for the future of our country if today's youth should ever become the leaders of tomorrow, because this youth is unbearable, reckless—just terrible."

Thirdly: "Our world has reached a critical stage; children no longer listen to their parents; the end of the world cannot be far away."

Finally: "This youth is rotten from the very bottom of their hearts; the young people are malicious and lazy; they will never be as youth happened to be before; our today's youth will not be able to maintain our culture."

The first came from Socrates, 470–399 B.C.; the second from Hesiod, *circa* 720 B.C.; the third from an Egyptian priest about 2,000 years B.C.; and the last was discovered recently on clay pots in the ruins of Old Babylon, and these were more than 3,000 years old.

Faced with these criticisms one could say that neither youth itself nor the world in general has done too badly in managing to maintain any worthwhile existence at all over the past 3,000 years. One would have thought that by now civilisation would have deteriorated to the point at which it was no longer endurable. Yet such is far from the case. Even in the past two decades when civilisation—or what we like to describe as civilisation in the western world—has had to resist greater and more determined onslaught upon its physical, spiritual, moral and traditional existence than in any other recorded period of time, quite a bearable fraction of it still remains.

The second point I think one must make in the face of these criticisms of the younger generation is that any writer today might be advised to think twice before adumbrating too fiercely upon the evil-doings and odd behaviour of today's youth.

And the third lesson we might learn is that these criticisms came, in each case, from the older generations—the parents of those days—the "squares" of their age perhaps—as much impelled by a forgetfulness of their own youth as we see in the critics of today. In setting out to reprove and to judge their young, time has proved them to be as foolish and as inaccurate as some of their mid-twentieth century successors.

If I wished to bring these criticisms up-to-date I would not speak of adolescents in particular but would quote General Omar Bradley in his description of the age in which we live. He said: "With the monstrous weapon man already has, humanity is in danger of being trapped in this world by its *moral* adolescence. Our knowledge of science has clearly outstripped our capacity to control it. We have too many men of science; too few men of God. We have grasped the mystery of the atom and rejected the Sermon on the Mount. Man is stumbling through a spiritual darkness while toying with the secrets of life and death. The world has achieved brilliance without wisdom, power without conscience. Ours is a world of nuclear giants and ethical infants.

We know more about war than we know about peace, more about killing than we know about living. This is our twentieth century's claim to distinction and to progress."

Here, I submit, is stark reality. Harsh though this stricture may be it is into this sort of world that today's adolescent is born, in which we expect him to live, and with which we ask him to compete.

Let us then, against this background, examine the adolescent, his problems and his reactions.

First, medically, of course, adolescence represents an exciting age group. Surgically, perhaps less so—unless the removal of a normal appendix in the case of abdominal pain due to constipation can be called exciting. Most of these incidents are so treated in order to satisfy the parents and to avoid embarrassing a surgeon in the holidays.

With the progress of preventive medicine over the past two decades the pattern of morbidity has changed considerably. School doctors have become unused to coping with epidemics— even of influenza—and the large sanatoria, and the staff required to man them, have become redundant. Yet to rebuild to meet the more modest requirements in terms of beds today and the somewhat more sophisticated needs of the outpatient department, is a costly exercise. Our bed occupancy at the College in Winchester spread out over the whole term varies from thirteen to twenty out of a total of 650 boys.

Yet the epidemic can still emerge. A year ago we came face to face with anictericic infective hepatitis at St. Swithun's School. There is no doubt that this disrupted the school programme more than any previous epidemic within my knowledge. A mass exercise with gamma globulin was effective—particularly in preventing the disease from leaping over the school holidays during the incubation period and starting again the next term— as we knew had happened in another school. As in other directions, in illness the adolescent tends not to do things by halves. The consolation is that in the same way that he will quite suddenly become very ill he fortunately makes a point of recovering at the same speed.

Adolescents are rarely seen in hospitals—this is perhaps as well, for the provisions in hospital for the care of adolescents are in the main inappropriate—they are, for example, particularly out of place in a general ward of a hospital, a high proportion of beds in which are taken up by geriatric patients; and the lack of availability of psychiatric beds for this age group in special units is a matter for concern.

The paediatrician's upper limit is aged thirteen; the next age group most often needing the help of the specialist is the middle aged—with their pregnancies, coronaries, duodenal ulcers and psychiatric problems. In between lies this group of adolescents—they represent what I think is happily phrased "the years between."

I have had it said to me more than once that all they need is the orthopaedic surgeon and the psychiatrist. Up to a point one agrees—adding, of course, the otorhinolaryngologist even though one has the impression that today he is called on much less frequently than of old.

Adolescents are notoriously bad history-givers. This is not deliberate. Aches and pains have no place in their lives, they are not used to being unfit or of interpreting or even remembering the signs and symptoms of a disability; they will, for example, ignore the pain associated with a slipped femoral epiphysis because of the importance of a house football match and they will return to active exercise (often with the encouragement of a housemaster or mistress and a team captain) long before they are fit to do so after an illness or injury.

They have, too, a rooted and particularly strong objection to and, I think, a subconscious fear of anything mysterious and unfamiliar. They like to think they are in control of their own destinies. Handing over to the doctor represents the passing of control, already unwillingly given to the schoolmaster, to the doctor. He is merely another type of authority—equally, if not more, to be avoided.

The result is that one can fall into the most awful traps unless one first has a good look at the patient—for his appearance will often give the game away—and then conducts a complete examination—no matter how unnecessary the latter may appear to be. It will seem, for example, that they have genuinely not noticed the rash of erythema nodosum or even a Henoch Schönlein purpura; that although their leg ached a bit they had no idea it was so tender in one particular spot, and so on. I accept that this can happen in any age group. I am emphasising that it can happen more dramatically and dangerously in adolescence.

Similarly, with the menstrual irregularities of the female. A wise school doctor knows that the great majority of these can be ignored (providing that anxious parents allow him to ignore them). Moreover, girls do not like talking about their periods even to their best friends or their house matrons. The vital point here is to *know* that there is an irregularity existing, to judge the occasional one in which investigation is required, to follow up a number unobtrusively—and to leave the rest alone. Even so, there will almost certainly be one or two who will escape notice simply because neither parent nor school are in the picture at all—and it is not unknown for a parent to ask a doctor to see a girl because she seems "run down" and for him to find that the cycle is fourteen days and the loss particularly heavy for the first two days. It may seem surprising that in the history taking the girl will make no mention of this unless pressed to talk about it.

Another point I wish to emphasise is that stress and strain can hit this age group as hard, if not harder, than others. Here, again, there is danger because the patients may be unaware of this themselves, the descent from being quite mentally fit and well to a point verging on collapse in some form or another may be so slow that it goes unnoticed. Here I cannot enlarge on this except to mention the need for an early warning by parents or school of any change in adolescent behaviour—withdrawal, insomnia, lack of appetite, irritability or the falling off in standards of work.

Most fortunately, schools which are almost bound nowadays to drive their pupils to achieve higher and higher standards (not only so that they can compete in examinations and win their places in Universities, but also so that the reputation of the School can be maintained) are aware of the problem and are usually very sympathetic to the individual boy or girl who finds it increasingly difficult to cope. Parents, too, share in the urging on of their young to work hard. This is more than understandable—yet I have heard parents talking in a way that has made me feel desperately sympathetic to a particular boy or girl who is literally pedalled round from school to school or university to university to gain a scholarship or even a place. As a doctor, one wonders whether this sort of traumatising is justifiable.

So that, in addition to the early warning one relies on from parent or school I am convinced that a consultant psychiatrist should be available at any moment to join the school doctor or general practitioner in the care of an adolescent. The present National Health Service machinery is inadequate and, even, inappropriate. This is not the psychiatrist's fault—there are too few of them and too few resources available to them.

Finally I commend to you what I call the "bolt-hole" bed. All schools and all Universities—indeed, all homes—should have one or two of these into which an adolescent can retreat without shame or recrimination for twenty-four to forty-eight hours. He or she must know that these beds exist and that they can be used at any time and without previous notice or reporting "sick". The occupant will be fed and kept warm and, otherwise, left alone. These beds act as a wonderful safety valve and I am so pleased to find that more and more schools and University Medical Centres are providing them. There is no need at all for the doctor to be drawn in at this stage. Only after forty-eight hours, if the bed is still occupied, need he be told.

What about the parents of today, for they represent the first of the adolescent's problems. (I must, of course, suppress some of the school doctor's unnatural thoughts about them, for there are times when a school doctor just does not like parents.)

In the majority it must be said that parents are a good lot, at least in their intentions if not so much in experience and training. They are loving and kind and ready and willing and they fall over backwards day after day trying to understand the most un-understandable phenomenon of any age—their adolescent offspring. Yet, with or without experience and training or any knowledge of what they are doing, by just being loving and just being where they are—and being *together* where they are—they are solving a majority of adolescent problems and preventing many more. By "loving" I do not mean over-indulging or spoiling—just "caring for" can be enough in itself; by "being there together" I do not mean at times or when it is thought necessary, but always. I believe and am always likely to believe (and this belief is based on experience as a parent and as a school doctor) that the foundation upon which adolescent behaviour is built is the home from which the adolescent emerges. Or, if you like to put it another way, adolescence does not create an image, it mirrors it.

What is the mirrored image today—as we see it reflected from the columns of newspapers and the screens of television sets? It must surely be one based on "Don't do as I do, just do as I say." If not, how can adults who marry and divorce each other, or indulge in uninhibited sexual experiences, criticise their young if they prefer not to come home or to be equally promiscuous. The indignity of sex today is primarily a product of adult—not adolescent—abuse. If that is what today's civilisation wants, that is what it has got.

Similarly, with alcohol, smoking and drug taking. Who are we to stand over our young and criticise them?

I would not like to be misunderstood in what I am saying; I do not for one moment suggest that I should judge so-called sexual immorality, the drinking of alcohol, the smoking of cigarettes or the swallowing of barbiturates and tranquillisers. I am merely saying "look out". There is a beam the size of an oak tree in the adult eye. Beware, therefore, of too concentrated an attack on the youthful mote.

If I might illustrate from a personal experience: as an adolescent I, in company with seven other boys, purloined the director of science's two-seater Morris from school premises, drove it to London and round Cambridge Circus the wrong way, knocked over a policeman dutifully stooping to read the front number plate and ended up in Bow Street. In retrospect this was an experience that I would assuredly not have missed and it certainly contained within it an intake of alcohol which would turn today's breathalyser green.

What am I to say, therefore, when a housemistress informs me that my elder daughter (now, incidentally, a most dutiful and imaginative mother of three) was seen playing games on the roof and escaping by means of the fire shoot, with the commendable result that she is now knitting dish cloths for the rest of the term. Am I to hold up my hands in horror and forget the impetuosity of youth or am I to conjure up a glimmer of understanding and the faint wisp of a reminiscent smile? Understanding is surely part of "caring for".

Shall we contrast this with the parents who write to a Housemaster and ask him to tell Jimmy that they are separating. Apart from the usurpation of responsibility—and one has to accept this today and the encouragement from the Welfare State which goes hand in hand with it—there is a lack of sensibility here which just does not understand how this sort of thing—even carefully presented—can tear a young boy or girl apart.

Both parents are loved; how can the home and the treasured belongings be divided into two; where is he or she to be sent next holidays; who is he or she to turn to for help and advice; what is to be faced or forced upon them in the future? This is probably the most unhappy and potentially dangerous adult image. Yet it is increasingly common and with the rising divorce rate a greater number of young people are deprived of the comfort and security that united parenthood can give them. A united family unit can meet and conquer the worst of adolescent crises, whilst a divided family may be unaware that a crisis exists.

I know there are many parents who stay together just for the sake of their children, others who find it impossible to remain under the same roof and a third group—probably the smallest— who show such a lack of discipline and such self indulgence that it is probably better for the sake of their young that they *should* separate; yet, in any case, there must inevitably be trauma to the young, varying from the moderate to the severe. And the young neither asked for it nor expected it; they were, one might say, born into it.

Apart from parents, what are some of the other factors responsible for the much-advertised behaviour of today's adolescents? We might first ask if there is much in "home" for some of them. One sitting room with a television set. Father wants one programme, the children another. Mother cannot stand loud pop music on the gramophone. So out the children go, wandering aimlessly in the streets. If by chance they cause distress in something they do they *could* be said merely to be getting their own back on their parents. Putting up a herdlike defence against a common enemy.

Similarly, it must not be forgotten that the young have few belongings of their own. The home and furniture, for example, are owned by their parents who, in middle age, have accumulated many of their own possessions. Adolescents, therefore, have little sense of property.

Social pressures have changed. Once upon a time what might be called "respectability" was the pattern—particularly in the smaller communities. To an increasing extent this is now going.

Nor can it be denied, I think—and it may be fair to attach this to any era—that with the higher education today it is inevitable that some parents feel a sense of inadequacy or inferiority; conversely, it is not difficult for children to guess at, take advantage of, or even be ashamed or worried about the supremacy they undoubtedly have in this respect over the older generations. When the younger is seen to advantage over the older, a tactful understanding on both sides is required—whether it be father and son, master and boy, foreman and apprentice or employer and employee. We cannot wonder that in this respect alone a misunderstanding and a frustration builds up, the impact of which is seen to be greater in the young, though the occult bitterness of the middle-aged may be the more dangerous. So that "being proud of" is part of "caring for."

Then we have, to my mind, the unfortunate denigration of things spiritual which must have succeeded in adding to adolescent insecurity and has deprived the young of one of the fixed moorings to which they could anchor their emotions. There is today the "changing face of fear"; we no longer believe in hell and punishment for sin. Yet the sanction from the spiritual side could be something better than this. It could, for example, work for a sense of community and individual responsibility.

At one stage in the preparation of this paper I collected together about a dozen of all sorts of adolescents. There were some who were "digging" round Winchester Cathedral, some members of youth clubs and some just curious. I did this really because I was anxious not to put over only my own idea of adolescence. We talked for hours about many things. On the whole they did not smoke or drink alcohol—this was not necessarily because they could not afford it but more probably because adults do both—which gives them an immediate disinclination to do either.

They all accepted that man had a spiritual, supersensory, other-worldly side and that this had to be catered for. They all, to my surprise, believed in a God—or, at any rate, a Supreme Being of some sort. None of them was a Christian but they were not intolerant to Christianity and they accepted Christ as a good chap with sensible ideas. They also accepted Mohammed, Buddha and Brahma (to mention only a few). The one thing of which they were certain (and I was not surprised) was that they themselves would search out and find their individual answer without any help from me. They were at pains to explain that I in my day accepted Christianity passively because I had it rammed down my throat from birth until I reached my University, when for the first time, I was allowed to think for myself; that I loved my neighbour because I was told to; that I failed to commit adultery (so far as they knew) because the fifth chapter of the Gospel of St. Matthew warned me against it.

They made a number of comments about my neighbour's ox and his ass, his maidservants and manservants and all the lustful thoughts and acts I might have committed against any or all of them, until I began to realise that it was not only parents and housemasters who thought me the lowest form of animal life; yet their thesis, and what they were trying to tell me, was that they were prepared to accept all these restrictions and to abide by all that was said in the Sermon on the Mount provided that they were allowed to make the decisions themselves; these being based on their own experience and learning of what was right and what was wrong, what good and what bad, what to be preserved and what ignored.

It is difficult not to admire this thesis. And not to accept it. Even though one could easily argue against it. Superficially it is rational and in the long term it should be far more durable and lasting. And I have seen it in action. Winchester Cathedral is full of adolescents every hour of every day of every month. They are in the majority not Christians. They are searching. They are judging. And I would add that many of my elderly and solitary patients are visited weekly by young boys and girls who voluntarily spend their spare time giving companionship and excitement to their "neighbours".

I can remember, too, with what relief I greeted my University and the sudden release from the awful bind of involuntary attendance at school chapel and choir practice; to a worship of a Trinity which I could not then understand and in which I could not believe. Are we, then, to condemn the young today because they will not tolerate this inexcusable hypocrisy? They believe in a God and in the spirit of man. We should leave them alone to learn how best and when to love their neighbours and how many of our ten imposed commandments should be observed *not only by them but by us as well.* Guiding them unobtrusively and trusting them is part of "caring for."

Arnold Toynbee, in *The Times* of April 5th, 1969, concluded an article on "Christianity's chance to triumph over Technology" with this paragraph :

> We are now moving into an age in which the range of choice will be wider and the exercise of the freedom to choose will become more frequent. We can look forward to a coming stage in mankind's religious history at which a person's religion will normally be not the one he has inherited, but the religion he has chosen *for himself* when he has come of age— a religion which may or may not be the one in which he has been born and brought up. This is a spiritual gain for future generations of mankind that has already been brought within sight by the change of heart which has overtaken the adherents of the diverse historic religions in our time.

Returning to the more mundane : there are some more factors we must consider in relation to today's adolescent behaviour : puberty is earlier, therefore emotional stress is earlier. In contrast, the school leaving age is later and the young find it difficult to reconcile the monastic existence of school life—and this particularly applies to boarding schools—with the permissiveness of the society in which they live outside school. It is vital that school authorities should recognise this situation and take steps to meet it. Similarly, parents in particular and society in general must accept it.

I am one who believes that sex education should start early and should be a continuing process. I do not think it should be taken as a thing apart from the schools' normal teaching programme—it should be as much a part of it as mathematics or history. If, outside the school, the pill and termination of pregnancy are to be regarded as "norms", then it is rational inside the school to reach a clear understanding, from the age at which understanding is first possible, as to how males and females are made and as to what males and females may make. The greatest gap between one generation and the other today and the greatest lack of understanding is on this question of sex knowledge and sex behaviour. There is as much need for the education of parents as for education of children. Teachers and family doctors have a tremendous responsibility in this field.

Then, youngsters leaving school can earn high wages for unskilled work and they may end up with more money in their pockets than their parents. This means that they can afford to try out all sorts of attitudes and behaviour. Add to this the fact that those who have goods to sell and who advertise are only too well aware of the money in children's pockets—money which will not be saved or even well spent. They consider that it is fair game to persuade the young to get rid of their money and they set out by displays and by advertising to get their hands on it. Older people were never faced with such temptations. So, again, it is not the children's fault. There is, thus, an urgent need in schools for the young to be taught what *money* is all about and what means there are of using it besides spending it all in an unproductive market.

The advent of television may have made gogglers and addicts of *us*—it has made slaves of some adolescents who model their clothes, their moral attitudes and behaviour on what they see or hear on television.

Then we have increasing urbanisation and industrialisation; the physical separation of the mother from the children when she goes out to work, with the consequent importance and influence of the father deteriorating.

Finally, in every generation, it seems to have been impossible for those who reach middle age to remember that adolescence is essentially an age of experiment and adventure. As we grow older so we become increasingly rigid and we express distaste at the changing face of the adolescent world. This is, for example, not the first time that young people—or even their parents—have had long hair and "peculiar" clothes. I think it most interesting and rather alarming that we should ignore history and believe that these oddities are the invention of today's youth. In any case, nothing can be duller than the appearance of the male sex today—one hardly dare wear any coloured suiting other than black without a furtive glance lest we be creating adverse comment from our peers. Any slight modification of the rigid and damnably uninteresting normal is at once the object of gossip—one is, for example, judged as schizophrenic, homosexual or extreme left wing politically. All this, of course, is part of today's middle-aged civilisation : conform or bust.

The adolescent, sensibly, will have none of this. He rightly thinks it is all what he vividly describes as a "load of cod's wallop." In any case, he must be different. In some cases, his long hair and his dirty neck and his unusual clothes are hiding or compensating for some much more worrying and potentially dangerous and asocial manifestation within himself. To cut his hair, wash his neck or change his clothing too soon may be all that is necessary to release his hitherto controlled frustrations to everyone's disadvantage and regret, including his own. Leave him alone for long enough and, with inner victory achieved, he will one day appear as a good-looking, highly respectable and rigidly conforming member of the commuter society. The alternative, if physically possible, is to grow one's own hair long and to buy one's own clothes in Carnaby Street. Within a week his hair will be shorn to the scalp and he will, at his parent's expense, be visiting Saville Row. If we cannot tolerate him, at least let us understand what makes him tick. Yet toleration is part of "caring for."

I wonder if I may remind you of the magnificent letter quoted by Mr. J. D. R. McConnell in his book *ETON, how it works.*

It is written to a boy's mother by his housemaster on his fifteenth birthday. He says :

... the real purpose of this letter is to try and prepare you for an imminent change in the relationship between yourself and your son. The affectionate small boy who has quite justifiably been your pride and joy is about to undergo such a transformation that you may well begin to wonder whether you have mothered a monster—perhaps you have already started to wonder where you have gone wrong and what you have done amiss to deserve his new-found anger.

Do not despair. Ride out the storm. Be firm but affectionate. At this moment when he seems to need you least he in fact needs you most. Make a stand about the principles you regard as fundamental. Give him rope about the less important things. Do not worry too much about his wearing apparel or the length of his hair. Comfort yourself with the knowledge that his present moods are transitory.

If you do this and stand firm as a rock in the midst of his tempestuous life the small boy whom you thought you had lost will return to you as a charming young man—well groomed in appearance and with delightful manners. He will have been worth waiting for.

Meanwhile we are both of us in for one hell of a time.

Again, in the days remembered by some of us, adolescents were given machine guns, taught how to use them and then told to go and shoot a man dressed up as an enemy—a German, for example, or an Italian. This was exciting and infinitely rewarding. It had an end product. Today, with no such opportunities, they provide themselves with long poles and attach large cards to them supporting or denigrating whatever happens to be the current or available good or bad cause. There is little excitement in this. It is relatively unrewarding and one may have to wait years for the end product—by which time it is no longer of any interest. Nor can one really talk about it in pubs or clubs for years afterwards.

One could never suggest that to make today's adolescent happy one should create a war for him to fight. But one must, on the contrary, draw from this picture the inevitable conclusion that for our eager adolescents today there is little for them to find but mischief of their own making and we should not too eagerly curse them for the drab society which we have created and in which we expect them to live. Many people, realising this only too well, are opening up new ventures in which adolescents can play and use their energy to a positive, good and exhausting effect. But our help is needed.

The Dean of King's College, London, Canon Sydney Evans, in his address during a service in Westminster Abbey commemorating the fiftieth anniversary of the Royal Air Force, said:

> The new tyrannies are latent in the rapid escalation of world population, in the world complex of inter-racial antipathies and in the depersonalising pressures of modern urban life. Are not the protests of the young the feeling that instead of living our own lives our lives are being lived for us; that "the system" has us in its grip; that we are expendable and replaceable like old cars; that decisions are made by faceless authorities we cannot reach? Secular achievement carries with it secular despair. The ambiguities of war have become the ambiguities of peace. This is our human condition and predicament. In our success lies our failure. Drugs are no remedy for the individual who finds himself alone in a rapidly changing world. Sexual tittilation on sale in glossy magazines is no remedy for the mounting boredom of suburbia —the loneliness of the bedsitter.
>
> The battles of the future will be battles of the mind, battles of the soul, battles for those interior and exterior freedoms without which a human being ceases to be a real person ... what kind of society are we actually getting in our western world ... and who calls the tune? ... *and who gets killed?*

What, then, should we do to help? In the first place I believe that young people are themselves looking round for security and leadership; finding no astronauts, no moon rockets, Nelsons or Churchills: few sportsmen or explorers on whom they can expend their emotions, they are creating their own standards, forming their own societies and throwing up their own heroes. These may not fit in with our ideas of what a standard of a hero should be, but at least we must accept that they are trying to fill a gap we have opened.

Next, with our moaning and groaning and our anxieties we should do ourselves the credit of accepting that we have now the basic conditions on which we would wish a new society to be built—well fed, well clothed and well housed.

Then I think we must recognise that these are *our* young and it is primarily up to us—particularly we who are teachers and doctors—to understand and to help them.

In a South Coast town recently a magistrate asked a boy to explain why he had committed his crime. The answer was, "You wouldn't understand." A tragic comment. Yet here is the gulf revealed between the generations.

It may be that some of them want to go it alone—it is certain that a few of them have no alternative; it may be that they seem not to want to meet us or to understand our point of view. Unless we are very close to them we shall never know, for they will be the last to tell us. It is probable that we shall have to be prepared to go a long way out of our way to help them against a seemingly impenetrable wall of ingratitude and obstinacy and resentment. I am sure that we shall often be hurt—but we shall suffer less if we remember that we once existed inside this adolescent and that in a few years, and if we are prepared to press on for long enough—come what may—*we shall be plain for him to see in himself*. For that is how life goes on, and thus patience is part of "caring for."

In fact, today's adolescent still carries the satchel, now heavy with books, either borrowed or purloined in the majority from some known or unknown source. The weight of it hanging from the left shoulder creates a scoliosis or exaggerates an already appalling posture. The adolescent has a shinier morning face than ever we knew, for the majority enjoy school and run willingly towards it. The adolescent is discerning and inquisitive and remarkably conservative when one considers his superficial liberal outlook towards most of the incidents in his daily round and common task. He is still shy and sensitive to criticism of himself. He may kick a boy when he's down if someone happens to be with him at the time. But if he is alone and confident that no one is looking he will stoop down and pull the victim to his feet.

The boy wishes to be a man and the girl a woman. There is nothing strange in this. We were the same and so was Socrates and the unknown writer on the Babylonian jars. All they ask is that we do not mock at them on their journey and that *if* we are there to help them at least we will let them appear to be helping themselves, and thus let diplomacy be a part of "caring for."

It is all terribly difficult and complicated. Sometimes the end product is one of great sorrow but more often, I submit, of enormous pride. My own adolescent family has grown up and left home—we have spent many hours describing each other's failures and shortcomings during the years of growing up. As more secrets were disclosed I shuddered and winced at my inadequacies and failings as a parent. I have certainly learnt enough to realise that, in the same way that some children suffer because of their parents, others grow up into civilised and useful adults in spite of their parents—however well-meaning and affectionate the latter may be; and, of course, affection and good intentions *must* be part of "caring for"! The trouble is that one learns on one's own children and there is some satisfaction at passing the wincing and the shuddering on to them, as they in turn face the awful problem of parenthood.

I know that in propounding my thesis on adolescents I shall have shocked many people profoundly—particularly, I think, psychiatrists and teachers. All I would say by way of excuse is that I have lived my life for two decades surrounded by some hundreds of other people's children. I am infinitely grateful to them that they have kept me young, at least in heart. I owe it to them in return that I should attempt, even if in a philosophic and unscientific way, to explain them to their parents and to suggest that they have made, and are making, the most out of this present civilisation of ours—in spite of us.

Kahlil Gibran in *The Prophet* said :

Your children are not your children
They are the sons and daughters of Life's longing for itself.
They came through you but not from you.
And though they are with you yet they belong not to you.
You may give them your love but not your thoughts,
For they have their own thoughts.
You may have their bodies, but not their souls,
For their souls dwell in the house of tomorrow, which you cannot visit, not even in your dreams.
You may strive to be like them, but seek not to make them like you.
For life goes not backward nor tarries with yesterday.

In conclusion, I leave you with two thoughts :

G. K. Chesterton said, "The only man who understood me was my tailor who measured me afresh each time we met." When dealing with adolescents may I suggest that you measure them afresh each time you meet them—whether they be pupils or patients, sons or daughters, and no matter how short the interval between the meetings.

And then, perhaps, we can take some consolation from Oscar Wilde, who said, "Children begin by loving their parents; as they grow older they judge them; sometimes they forgive them."

These observations about adolescents formed the basis of a medical lecture given by Dr. Gibson in Portsmouth and subsequently published in the *British Medical Journal* and in the Headmasters' Conference journal *Conference*.

Appendix I

Some Useful Addresses

BIRMINGHAM

The Open Door
(Correspondence) 101 Gough Road, Birmingham, B15 2JG.
Tel : 440 1472 or 472 5975 after 5 p.m.
(Walk-in) 161 Corporation Street.

Offers an opportunity for young people living in and around
Birmingham to consult a knowledgeable adult in private and
anonymously if they wish. There is a wide range of specialised
consultants.

BRISTOL

Off the Record—a consultation service for young people,
7 Berkeley Square, Bristol, BS8 1HG.

CAMBRIDGE

Cambridge Advisory Centre for Young People, 11 Benny's Way,
Coton, Cambs.

CHELTENHAM

Contact—Advisory and Information Service, 15 Rodney Road,
Cheltenham, Glos. GLS0 1HX.

COVENTRY

Richmond Fellowship Halfway House, Verecroft, 20 Davenport Road, Coventry. Tel : 0203 7673
Initially for fifteen residents of both sexes between ages fifteen and twenty. Priority given to Coventry and Midlands.

EXETER

Young People's Consultation Centre, 2 Waterbeer Street, Exeter.
Offers young people the opportunity to discuss personal problems and to obtain help for them when necessary.

GLOUCESTER

Young People's Advice Service, 29 Barnwood Avenue, Gloucester.
A centre for young people looking for help and information.

LEAMINGTON SPA

Young People's Advisory Service, 49a The Parade, Leamington Spa, Warwick.

LIVERPOOL

M.Y.P.A.C. (Merseyside Young People's Advisory Clinic, in affiliation with Brook Advisory Centres).
Clinics held at :
63 Walton Road, Liverpool, L4 4A (Thursday evenings). Tel : 051-207 3456 (Mornings only).
Gambier Terrace, Liverpool L1 7BG. Tel : 051-709 4558.

LONDON

Off the Record, 313 Ballards Lane, Tally Ho Corner, Finchley, N.12. Tel : 445 0888 (Monday to Friday for appointment).

Young People's Consultation Service, Tavistock Centre, Adolescent Unit, 120 Belsize Lane, N.W.3.

Virgin Records, 10 South Wharf Road, W.2. Tel: 402 5231.

Brent Centre for Study of Adolescents, 51 Winchester Avenue, London N.W.6.

C.U.R.E., National Addiction Research Institute, 533A King's Road, (Lots Road entrance), London SW10 0TZ. Tel: 352 1590.

Richmond Fellowship Halfway House, Argyll Lodge, 20 Argyll Road, Kensington, London W.8. Tel: 937 0607.

For fourteen young adults of both sexes and all diagnoses.

Release, 1 Elgin Avenue, London W.9. Tel: 289 1123.

Legal help, advice on drugs, abortion, civil rights. Also offer psychiatric aid. They have a full-time psychiatric social worker and a doctor and/or psychiatrist on Monday and Thursday evenings till 22.00. If problem is serious they refer people to Middlesex or Maudsley Hospitals where there are sympathetic departments. For drug "busts" and related problems emergency number: 289 1123.

Brook Advisory Centres.

Set up to give contraceptive advice to unmarried people between the ages of sixteen and twenty-five. For clinics in the London area enquiries to 233 Tottenham Court Road, London W.1. Tel: 580 2991.

P.N.P. (People not Psychiatry).

A scattered group of young people who are all suffering in some way or another, but with some others who wish to help. They help one another with their problems. P.N.P. publish a list of members. Contact address: 62b Savernake Road, London N.W.3. Tel: 486 9370.

LUTON

The Young People's Advisory Service, Central Library, Bridge Street, Luton.

Gives confidential advice to any young person on any problem.

MANCHESTER

Young People's Advice Centre, 50 Bridge Street, Deansgate, Manchester, 21.

Gives short term counselling and referral to appropriate agencies where necessary.

OXFORD

Richmond Fellowship Halfway House, Rutland House, 41 Davenant Road, Oxford. Tel: 0865 55127.

For fifteen full-time students of both sexes and all diagnoses. Other young adults considered if there are vacancies.

PORTSMOUTH

Young People's Consultation Centre, 3 All Saints Street, Portsmouth (known as "Help for your Problem").

RICHMOND

Youth Counselling Clinic, Health Clinic, King's Road, Richmond. Tel: 940 9761.

Richmond Fellowship Halfway House, Lancaster House, 22 Lancaster Park, Richmond.

For seventeen adolescents and young adults of both sexes and all diagnoses; mostly short stay residents (six to twelve months). Priority given to those from the London Borough of Richmond.

SALISBURY

"Johnathons", 88 Milford Street, Salisbury, Wilts.
Helps young people with family, personal, or social problems.

SHEFFIELD

Sheffield Young People's Consultation Centre, 408 Eccleshall Road, Sheffield.
Helps young people with personal problems and provides professional advice for those with emotional and sexual problems.

SOUTHAMPTON

Hamton Advisory Centre, 70 Manor Farm Road, Southampton. Tel: Southampton 57934.
Richmond Fellowship Halfway House, Bracken House, Chilworth, Southampton. Tel: Southampton 67154.
For eighteen adolescent girls (age fourteen to twenty) of all diagnoses. Priority given to Leigh House Adolescent Treatment Centre and to applications from Hampshire.

WOLVERHAMPTON

Young People's Telephone Advisory Centre sponsored by Wolverhampton Education Authority.
Offers young people opportunity to discuss personal problems.

In case of change of address of any of the above organisations or for any further information apply the Youth Service Information Centre, The National College for the Training of Youth Leaders, Humberstone Drive, Leicester, LE5 0RG.

Appendix II

For Further Reading

Words, Jean-Paul Sartre (Penguin, 1965)

The Urgency of Change, Krishnamurti (Gollancz, 1971)

The Divided Self, R. D. Laing (Tavistock Publications, 1960)

The Delinquent Solution, David Downes (Routledge and Kegan Paul, 1965)

Identity: Youth and Crises, Erik H. Erikson (Faber and Faber, 1968)

I and Thou, M. Buber (T. and T. Clark, 1960)

The Family and Individual Development, D. W. Winnicott (Tavistock Publications, 1965)

Fact and Fiction in Psychology, H. J. Eysenck (Penguin, 1965)

The Naked Ape, Desmond Morris (Jonathan Cape, 1967)

The Permissive Society, John Wilson (Panther, 1969)

The Wedding Guest Syndrome, Roy Ridgway (New Doctor, Professional Research Publications, 1969)

New Pathways in Psychology, Colin Wilson (Gollancz, 1972)

Adolescence, Cyril Smith (Longmans Green, 1968)

Bomb Culture, Jeff Nuttall (MacGibbin and Kee, 1968)

Male and Female, Margaret Mead (Pelican Books, 1962)

Playpower, Richard Neville (Jonathan Cape, 1970)

Index

Aggression in Youth